EXODUS

A Hermeneutics of Freedom

J. Severino Croatto

*Translated from the Spanish
by Salvator Attanasio*

WIPF & STOCK · Eugene, Oregon

Wipf and Stock Publishers
199 W 8th Ave, Suite 3
Eugene, OR 97401

Exodus
A Hermeneutics of Freedom
By Croatto, J. Severino and Attanasio, Salvator
Copyright © 1981 Orbis Books All rights reserved.
Softcover ISBN-13: 978-1-6667-1860-7
Hardcover ISBN-13: 978-1-6667-1861-4
Publication date 4/21/2021
Previously published by Orbis Books, 1981

This edition is a scanned facsimile of the original edition published in 1981.

Contents

Preface to the Revised Edition   iv

I. In Quest of "Meaning"   1
    1. PRELIMINARY ORIENTATION   1
    2. BIBLE AND "LIBERATION"   3
    3. LIBERATION AND FREEDOM   4
    4. A "SIGN OF THE TIMES"?   6
    5. PLAN OF THE ANALYSIS   10

II. Exodus: Event and Word   12
    1. THE EXODUS AS "RESERVOIR-OF-MEANING"   12
    2. FROM THE EVENT TO THE WORD   13
    3. FROM THE EVENT TO THE PROMISE   15
    4. ANALYSIS OF THE SITUATION   16
    5. THE WORD THAT PRECEDES LIBERATION   18
    6. THE EVENT OF LIBERATION   23
    7. THE HERMENEUTICAL ACCOUNT   25
    8. THE MESSAGE   27

III. Created for Freedom   31
    1. THE ESSENCE AND TRANSCENDENCE OF HUMAN BEINGS   31
    2. HUMANKIND'S MISSION IN THE WORLD   33
    3. THE MYTHICAL WORLDVIEW   34
    4. THE BIBLICAL WORLDVIEW   34
    5. FROM THE IDEAL TO THE REALIZATION   35
    6. SOME REFLECTIONS   36

IV. The Prophet, "Conscientizer" of Alienated Humanity   39
    1. THE PROPHET, "CRITIC" OF ISRAEL   41
    2. THE PROPHET, "CONSCIENTIZER" OF THE PEOPLE   43
    3. THE PROPHET, INTERPRETER OF HISTORY   45
    4. PROPHECY AND POLITICS   46

V. The Christ, "Liberator" of the Oppressed   48
    1. FROM THE MESSIAH TO THE SUFFERING SERVANT   48
    2. THE "LIBERATING" ATTITUDES OF JESUS   49
    3. THE "CONSCIENTIZING" WORD OF JESUS   52
    4. THE ANNOUNCEMENT TO THE POOR   55
    5. THE "LIBERATING" DEATH OF JESUS   57
    6. CHRIST AND THE LAW   65

VI. Paul: Radical Human "Liberation"   67
    1. THE TRIPLE ALIENATION   68
    2. THE THREE ALIENATIONS, ACCORDING TO ROMANS 5-7   71
    3. FROM DEATH TO LIFE   74
    4. OUR PASCHAL LIBERATION   76
    5. HERMENEUTICS OF "PASCHAL" LIBERATION   79
    6. CONCLUSION   82

Notes   83

Scriptural Index   87

Preface to the Revised Edition

This essay in hermeneutics, written and published more than five years ago, now appears in a second revised edition. The very nature of hermeneutic discourse rules out its being fixed in final form once and for all. It must undergo constant re-readings in the light of processes that bring the meaning out of hiding. This is not to suggest that theology is fickle, and hence superficial. Precisely because theology is supposed to carry the search for God deeper, it must know how to lay hold of God in concrete happenings and express God's epiphany in a discourse that is ever new.

The aim of my reflections in this book is to contribute a few epistemological elements to the theology of liberation. The theme itself is important, of course, because it is the core of the biblical message. But my main stress is on *how* the kerygma of liberation is treated as a theme in the Bible; this is taken as our model for the hermeneutic process. In discovering the possibilities for re-reading the Exodus, I am not suggesting that we talk only about the Exodus. Quite the contrary is the case. I am trying to show how this can generate new happenings with their corresponding readings.[1] If we take the Exodus as our theme, we do so because in it Latin American theology finds a focal point of the first magnitude and an inexhaustible light.

At this stage in our historical process some try to give the impression that we should not be talking about a theology of liberation but rather about a theology of "captivity"; or else that we should simply go back to classical theology. There are ill-intentioned efforts to bring liberation theology into disrepute by those who do not want the real liberation of Latin America.[2] Some fear that a so-called anthropological emphasis will work to the detriment of "revelation" and the work of God. In the face of such threats, the need to go more deeply into the methodology of the theme of liberation becomes all the more urgent.[3]

Is it correct to say that the theology of exile should now come to the forefront in our reflection? For that to be true, the theology of exile cannot be merely an extension of the theology of liberation.[4] The change in perspective can be useful if we want to avoid any premature triumphalism, if we want to take better cognizance of the suffering and martyrdom implied in our present captivity. But even that indicates that the important thing is not captivity but liberation from it. The theology of the Exodus is not simply something "after" the salvific event—the more distant our reading is from the original event, the greater its capacity to enrich the meaning of that event.[5] Rather, it is a contextual "after" which awakens the "memory" of that event because the people are again oppressed or afraid of being oppressed. Liberation is not celebrated as a mere act of triumphal thanksgiving but as an acknowledgment of faith in the liberating God who can still liberate. We might note in passing, for example, the extent to which Deutero-Isaiah uses the theologoumenon of the "new Exodus"—not as a literary image but primarily as a key for hope.[6] So a theology of liberation is a theology of the process of liberation, not of achieved liberty. Today that process contains more shadows than it did a few years ago; but in the last analysis it is a process, not a captivity without hope. To avoid confusion, we should get rid of the term "theology of captivity" and realize that a theology of liberation is carried out from within a state of oppression (and the changing stages of the liberation process) rather than from a situation of freedom.

The accusation that liberation theology is excessively anthropological comes from classical theology, which possesses a God already "locked up" in the Sources who is the object of a distant faith. Leaving aside the fact that such a faith is more ideological than belief in the biblical God of history, I should like to make two observations that have to do with the theme of this book. First of all, the biblical God is not the God of the Sources (an object of study and of reason) but the God-of-history of which the Sources speak to us as a kerygmatic "memory" that sheds light on the God in action now. The biblical message wells up from the salvific happening—this is the hermeneutic key I shall hark back to again and again. The salvific happening is the point of departure for theology, and the latter in turn must be reformulated as the discourse of faith on the ever new manifestations of God in history.[7] Secondly, as I explain in section 5 of Chapter II, faith reads God at work in history. But the supposition is that this history is human history, not some special history for Christians. In other words, *human* events must be deciphered as the locale of *God's* revelation. So when the theology of liberation stresses the function of praxis as a theological locus, it is not supplanting God with the human being; it is simply "seeking God" (to use a prophetic expression that is fraught with hermeneutic content)[8] in the one and only place where God's epiphany takes place in human life. So if we wish to identify the liberating God who still saves us today, we will be hard put to find God outside the *human* processes of liberation. And that is an act of faith, which Chapter II in this book tries to get across.

From another standpoint some European theologians criticize the originality of the theology of liberation without being opposed to it themselves.[9] No one can deny that much of the conceptual baggage of liberation theologians is European in origin; but that does not make their theological discourse a dependent, derivative line of thinking. Why? Because theirs is a contextual discourse, not a universal one; and also because it has been worked out in the praxis of liberation stemming from a situation of dependence that is specifically ours. Now more than ever before, Europeans will have to formulate their own theology of liberation on the basis of their own liberation processes. Yet, despite that fact, the epistemological change that Latin American liberation theology has injected dialectically into theological discourse is an irreversible achievement which is valid for other contexts as well. The best thing about it is the fact that "theology born of praxis" is not a Latin American novelty but the starting point for biblical theology itself. This fact is fraught with consequences that we wish to spell out.

The above remarks bring me back to what I indicated at the start as the intent of this work. I want to contribute to the epistemology of the theology of liberation, shoring it up against accusations of illegitimacy at the present time and, even more importantly, making it more fruitful. "Theology born of praxis" is precisely that: *theology*. It must speak about the God of history, and it must be continually collated with the biblical kerygma of liberation.

But how do we do this? Reading the signs of the times bears no similarity at all to any literal matching up of the Bible with some specific situation (see Chapter I, section 3); to look for resemblances is to remain on the exterior, superficial level. Authentic re-reading works from within. It links kerygma and situation along a semantic axis, disentangling an excess of meaning that is discovered to be such precisely because a *new* process or happening appears "within," without having been on the author's horizon of understanding. This is what is called "eisegesis," which enters into the text without being impertinent subjectivity.

So this little book seeks to orchestrate a method for re-reading the Bible from the standpoint of our own situation in Latin America. The aim of our method is to enable us to construct a *theology* of liberation and to avoid the opposite danger—the danger of flatly denying the relevance of the Bible, insofar as it is a text from the past, as a message of liberation *for us*.

CHAPTER I

In Quest of "Meaning"

1. PRELIMINARY ORIENTATION

This chapter title, like the special vocabulary used throughout the book, calls attention to our markedly Ricoeurian approach to philosophical and religious hermeneutics. It is appropriate for us to set forth certain presuppositions in order to clarify the essential meaning of the subject under discussion.

Hermeneutics is a branch of semiotics—while at the same time going beyond it. Hermeneutics is the science of understanding the meaning that human beings inscribe in their practices, as well as in their interpretation by word, text, or other practices. All human action becomes a sign to be decoded, and the reason for doing so is all the more compelling if it is God who inscribes a meaning in events. Among the hermeneutical principles we make use of are the following:

1. A human event does not exhaust itself simply by occurring, nor in the chronicle that describes it. It has the capacity to generate other happenings—what H. G. Gadamer calls the "historical effect."[1] We are not concerned with this phenomenon from the viewpoint of causality, but rather from the viewpoint of understanding. The meaning of the more recent event is found to be already included within the prior event. As the chain of events lengthens, its significance retrospectively accumulates in that remote starting point.

2. This phenomenon explains why certain occurrences establish themselves as foundational events, on the level of praxis, and as a reservoir-of-meaning on the level of understanding. They are not such from the outset, but become such because of their "historical effect." Thus some human events are submerged in obscurity, while others increase in luminosity insofar as other happenings are understood in their semantic axis.

3. The greater the distance between a foundational and a founded event,

the greater the density of the former's significance. This is the hermeneutical function of "distantiation" of which Ricoeur speaks in his more recent writings;[2] he applies this principle to the interpretation of texts (see principle 6 below). We shall see how distantiation operates in re-readings of the biblical book of Exodus.

4. The event precedes the word (see Chap. II, Secs. 2 and 3): the word interprets the event and unfolds its reservoir-of-meaning. The act of interpreting is simultaneously the act of accumulating meaning. When a word expresses the meaning of an event, it is giving meaning to the event. There is nothing paradoxical in this; it is rather the very essence of every moment of interpretation. Exegesis is eisegesis, and anybody who claims to be doing only the former is, wittingly or unwittingly, engaged in ideological subterfuge. Not even the physical sciences are exempt from this principle.

5. "Hermeneutic circularity,"[3] the round-trip itinerary entailed in the process of interpretation, is conditioned and made possible by the mutual illumination that occurs between the foundational event and the founded event, or between the foundational event and its word, or between exegesis and eisegesis. The primitive Church interpreted Jesus from the perspective of the Scriptures, but at the same time it interpreted the Scriptures from the perspective of the Jesus event. In fact, the event (Jesus) that generates the word (the New Testament) comes first; but the New Testament, in turn, was possible only as a re-reading of the Old Testament. These three aspects, subsumed in *one* kerygma (the Bible: the Old and New Testaments as interpretation of Christ) form a new pole of hermeneutic circularity that now includes us as its complementary pole. And so on and so on.

6. Utilizing the contributions of linguistics—with its distinction between language, speech (the act of speaking), and writing, or text—Ricoeur shows that just as language is superseded in discourse—in the act of speaking—discourse is in turn superseded in the production of the literary work. In discourse, the speaker and the hearer determine the meaning of the words they use, which in itself is polysemic. The frame of reference, for its part, is precise: one person speaks to another about something at a particular time and in a particular place.

All these elements are modified, however, when the meaning is inscribed in a text: the author is no longer present; the reader is not the person to whom the words were originally addressed; the frame of reference, or the "world of the text," is no longer the same. Accordingly a "distantiation" arises between the author of a work and its interpreter. The work turns out to be polysemic (in contradistinction to the act of speaking, or discourse, which closes off the meaning); it is now open to a new appropriation of its meaning.

Building on Gadamer's approach, Ricoeur elaborates the notion of the "world of the text," namely, those possible meanings of the text arising from its condition as linguistic "sign," superseding the phrase and becoming a codified structure or composition. For the interpreter, the "world of the text" is something "in front of the text," not something "behind" it, like the author.

It opens the text to an understanding from the vantage point of its new horizon. Note that traditional exegesis seeks to identify the meaning of a text by investigating what lies "behind" it (author, traditions, earlier literary forms); hermeneutics adds to this the understanding of the meaning that lies "in front" of the text.[4]

7. The practices of a group or of a community that occupies a specific territory are situated along the axis formed by the "foundational event" and the "historical project" (in other words, "memory" and "prophecy"). In one way or another this, consequently, gives rise to *conflict* of interpretation. There is a surplus-of-meaning in life and in all human praxis that is especially concentrated in the foundational and archetypical events that sustain a group's way of being. Social practices always signify, and intend to be, an *appropriation* of meaning. And any appropriation is agonic. Struggle—on the level of practices or on the level of symbolics—can arise at any moment of conscious human life. In every practice, something is born and something dies.

8. Division is a form of appropriation of meaning, which nobody can totally control (although claims to that effect are always being made!). History shows that the rise of new groups or traditions is the expression of an appropriation of meaning. Christianity itself was born of a conflict of interpretation: the practices of Jesus, and their accompanying words, were not interpreted as an innovation but as a recovery of the originating kerygma of Israel, coming into conflict with a pharisaic interpretation of that same kerygma. As we shall see, Jesus' problem was with the Jews and not with the Romans (the conflict of interpretation is generated within the frame of a commonly held symbolic vision and worldview). This phenomenon can be recognized in the political and ideological realms and indeed on every plane of human praxis—with their corresponding theories.

9. In the light of these presuppositions, briefly described here, we can speak of a circular dialectic between event and word, and, by the same token, between kerygma and situation, between the biblical word on liberation and our processes of liberation. But a hermeneutic reading of the biblical message occurs only when the reading *supersedes the first contextual meaning* (not only that of the author but also that of his first readers). This happens *through the unfolding of a surplus-of-meaning disclosed by a new question addressed to the text.*

These guidelines will help the reader to understand the lexicon used here and, above all, to grasp the purpose of the book. Because of what we have said, Chaps. II and VI cannot be separated from each other; they explicate each other and lead to the conclusion synthesized in Chap. VI, Sec. 5.

2. BIBLE AND "LIBERATION"

A discussion of the *biblical* theme of "liberation" presupposes in principle that there is a kerygmatic content: the Bible does not discuss "notions" but enunciates and announces a message. If the Bible discusses anything, it is to challenge human activities. Therefore, whenever we read an account of the liberation of the people of Israel, we are being instructed on a call to *us* and we are being prompted to embark upon a quest for the "meaning" of what God did and, therefore, "said" as Word. Nevertheless, we wish to point out that talking about the biblical idea of "liberation" is a very serious and hazardous business. We are holding an explosive Word in our hands: it "does" something, or it kills the one who does not use it.

"Liberation" is a much used word in our time, as was "salvation" *(soteria)* in the time of Christ. "Salvation" was one of the key words that summarized a whole worldview, not only in Palestine but also in the Hellenistic culture area. Another such term was "gnosis" in the first Christian centuries, and "humanism," "existentialism," and others in recent times. Now it is the turn of "liberation." Everybody uses it, everybody has to use it, even without understanding it, even to the point of interjecting it into an anti-liberational worldview. The word simply must be used in any and all ways if we want to be properly esteemed and not denounced as old fogies or reactionaries.

But when a key word, a worldview word, enters into general currency, it is bound to lose its intensity and its power to challenge. Again we see that the word is charged with meaning through *deeds*. The verse from the Gospel of Matthew (7:21) applies: "Not every one who says to me, Lord, Lord . . . but he who *does*. . . ." *Reality* alone will permit us to distinguish between those who "talk" of liberation and those who are involved in the liberation process.

"Liberation" is a word that nevertheless "speaks" and "says" a lot. It is a word full of hope because of the meaning it has borne from the time of its illumination in the story of the exodus. And it is full of hope because of the meaning with which it can be "charged" by genuine liberative deeds, especially in our Latin America, suffering from a long and painful captivity but conscious of the call to be a great liberated homeland.

We are taking for granted here the frame of reference indicated by the word "dependence," the antithetical correlate of "liberation."[5] The scope of the term "liberation," as "project," is wider, including antithetical correlates such as "alienation," "estrangement," "exile," egoism, law, death, and many others. One of the central intentions of this essay is to determine precisely what the biblical kerygma—as the word "signifying" the salvific events lived by Israel—makes explicit and precisely what it permits us to "explore" from our *own* perspective.

3. LIBERATION AND FREEDOM

It is easy to perceive a quest for freedom and an affirmation of freedom in the men and women of our day. In recent decades awareness of personal values has intensified in reaction to a tangle of mechanisms of oppression woven over the centuries. At times such oppression was inflicted in the name of religion itself, at other times in the name of a false "culture" that imposes oppressive rules of behavior or exalts secondary values, submerging the higher ones. We are all acquainted with the gamut of "paternalisms" (e.g., in the family or the State); "maternalisms" (e.g., the Church-structure as overprotective mother); colonialism of old countries over the new, of the richer countries over the poorer; of the many forms of social oppression (whites against blacks, bosses against workers, the powerful against those forsaken by the law, the privileged class against the bottommost strata, the mighty against the meek, etc.).

Injustices have existed in all times (the first known social reform, introduced by the Sumerian king Urukagina, reverts to 2600 B.C.). And in all times there have been attempts to achieve liberation. Such attempts are an expression of human history.

It is only in our era, however, that humanity has begun to attack oppression on all fronts: the social (by the blacks, the workers, the dispossessed classes), the political (by the poor nations kept in a state of underdevelopment, the marginalized sectors within each country), the cultural (against a typical form of colonialism), the psychological (especially by psychoanalysis), and, finally, the religious (by a rejection of both European and juridical norms on the structural level, and by an earnest assumption of history as space-of-faith on the level of Christian praxis).

The struggle of so many oppressed peoples who are seeking to "say their word," who desire to "be" what now they know they can be and must be, is perhaps the characteristic phenomenon of our time. There is new *value* placed on freedom; it is considered as a vocation "to be" with all the possibilities that we intuit in ourselves and in our moment in history. But at the same time we discover ourselves as "called to freedom," we also become conscious that we do not possess it—whether as individuals or as a people. In the face of both the danger of frustration and the attraction of that vocation, we initiate a *process* of liberation. Hence the important goal is not liberation, but freedom. The former is a process "toward" the latter, which is the ontological "locus" wherein human beings can be fulfilled. We shall see that the exodus is a deed of "liberation," but not the possession of freedom. The "departure" from Egypt is the first step toward the "entrance" to the Promised land. The struggles of our Latin American peoples are not a precondition for their being, but rather for their march toward real independence (which was merely "programmed" in the patriotic deeds of the 1800s).

The massive cry of humankind, which suddenly feels itself groaning under the human-made yoke of "being-of-another," now attains an unprecedented volume thanks to the new method of "conscientization" orchestrated by the social sciences and the mass media. The degree of maturity achieved by the people of our century does not permit them to attribute their ills to *fate;* rather the cause is ascribed to the egoism or to the lust for power of their fellows. Thus they know that their own "vocational" freedom is also their present "freedom" to set in motion their own process of liberation. This fact bears on the biblical reflection that we wish to make, especially when we treat of Genesis.

For the time being we point out that liberation "projects" are in progress all over the world; after all the scope of liberation is very broad, just as the subjections that humankind suffers are many. We do, however, find all the forms of "alienation" and of dependence with respect to the North Atlantic countries (Europe and the United States) concentrated, in a certain sense, in the Third World countries. Even "religious" dependence makes itself felt with a particular weight in the marginalized countries.

We hope that we have, in a few lines, adequately explained the relation between freedom and liberation.

4. A "SIGN OF THE TIMES"?

What we have treated in the preceding section gives rise to a hermeneutic question: Does not today's quest for *freedom* through humankind's many deeds of *liberation* represent a "favorable" moment (a *kairos,* according to the biblical lexicon) for action on the part of the Christian? In other words, what does this aforementioned phenomenon signify for those who read the Scriptures as message?

It was not Christians (in the sense of the "official" Church) who in our time were the first to "rediscover" freedom in its sociopolitical or psychological dimensions. On the contrary, in the economic order, it was the "western Christian" culture that gave birth to the oppressive "liberal" understanding of money and economic enterprise. The freedom that a juridical Church demanded was that permitting the profession of its faith, but with a strange mixture of oppressive intolerance toward other religious groups. As heir to Roman juridicism, Germanic imperialism, and medieval feudalism, the Church intensified an authoritarian verticalism that in principle "agreed" with the higher established authorities. "Freedom" continued being evaluated "in a vacuum," or in a closed circuit.

As a result the authentically human and Christian values of freedom were recovered outside the Church, or by Christian groups who felt that the Gospel inclined in other directions than those already exhausted by the moribund Church. (There were, of course, many exceptions.) As a general rule, changes are not introduced from above, especially by the oppressors.[6] People began to discover their vocation to freedom and to free themselves on the basis of their own lived experience of oppression. They were prompted by a process of conscientization elucidated by the philosophers of "suspicion" (Marx, Freud, Nietzsche),[7] but also accelerated by leading figures who themselves became symbols of liberation.

The grassroots Christian communities *(comunidades cristianas de base)* were the first to "tune in" on this voice of humanity "in a state of liberation." Thus a change of mentality occurred among Christians, namely, an acceptance of the values of freedom, notwithstanding its "perils" so often proclaimed in catechetics and sermons. This, in turn, entailed two fundamental things: freedom began to be considered as a *supreme value* of the Christian message, with a concomitant loathing for its concealment by a Christian ethic more oppressive than salvific; on the other hand, such a discovery connoted an "energizing" of Christians open to the Gospel.

These two aspects require amplification. From the "static" viewpoint of the traditional ethic, including its essential disorientation, the discovery of the value of freedom and of the call to act in the process of liberation signified a recovery of another essential datum of the biblical kerygma: that God reveals himself in the events of the world or of peoples, awakening the Christian conscience when it is somnolent or distracted. If God manifests himself in history, and not only in the Word already uttered, or if he shows himself in the events of the world in order to disassociate himself from the "monopoly of truth" that obscures and "suppresses" truth (Rom. 1:18), Christians begin to realize that the response to this God-of-history demands from them a commitment *in this history.* Therein lies the profound difference between praxis as a *human being* and praxis as a *Christian.* Once we discover God *in the event* through faith, God appears *much more* exigent than he does to those who have not discovered him there and who act on a merely human plane. That is one of the deepest meanings of the "Christian being," of "knowing" the conscientizing Word of God.

It is, however, on the basis of this process of discovery of the God-of-freedom, and not through a revelation extraneous to history, that we begin to grasp that what is most human is also most Christian. Biblical revelation does not emphasize superhuman values; instead, it "energizes" the quintessentially human values such as freedom, love, creativity, work, hope, etc. Adam is criticized for his supraontological pride, his desire to be god, not for his creativity, his love, or his freedom, which were given to him as a constitutive part of his proper vocation. Christ's central message, brotherly love, is not an unknown supra-value, but the maximum demand of what is maximally *human.* Freedom and love are the two great biblical themes, and they are also precisely the two great *human* values that permit the greatest fulfillment or beget the worst of frustrations.

Nevertheless the fact remains that the liberation processes demand more from the "conscientized" Christian than from the non-Christian. The same demand conditioned Israel with respect to other peoples: far from being a privilege, to be an Israelite required a commitment and a greater fidelity. The prophet Amos makes this very clear when he indicts Israel for its "licentiousness" in the name of its special vocation: "Are you not like the Ethiopians to me, O people of Israel? says the Lord. Did I not bring up Israel from the land of Egypt, and the Philistines from Caphtor [Crete?] and the Arameans from Kir [Assyria?]? Behold, the eyes of the Lord God are on the sinful kingdom, and I will destroy it from the surface of the ground" (9:7ff.). Philistines and Arameans were no longer in existence at the time of the prophet (eighth century B.C.) even though they had been led by Yahweh in their time. It is a warning for anyone who feels safe and smug in the possession of any improperly understood privilege. Paul also, in the letter to the Romans (1–11), speaks of the fall of the Jewish people that had considered itself superior to the pagans. God calls to humility those who think they possess the whole truth by manifesting himself in "other" places; or God demands a tremendous fidelity from those who have discovered him and to whom, on the other hand, he grants a special grace to accomplish a mission in the world.

In sum, once they have grasped the biblical mission of freedom as an essential vocation of humankind, Christians have an all the *greater* commitment to initiate a liberating process, or to collaborate with it.

The recognition of freedom as an evangelical value and the manner in which this recognition has occurred signifies that we are in the presence of a "sign of the times." There is no need to explain this expression of evangelical origin (Luke 11:56), so widely disseminated since John XXIII and Vatican II. It is possible, however, that it has become voguish before being understood in all its kerygmatic profoundity. To recognize the signs of the times, or to read the presence of God in the events of the world, requires at least a very deep "attunement" between these events and the Christian message.[8] But such attunement occurs first of all because God is discovered *in the event,* from which one goes back to the archetypical message as a guarantee of the fidelity of the meaning of the event and as a summons from the perspective of one's own faith. The opposite itinerary, on the other hand, can remain in a situational accommodation of the message to the present event, or, what is worse, prevent that the received message be enriched by the new manifestation of God in history and even have its superannuated interpretations be corrected.

This assertion anticipates an important hermeneutic reflection that we shall take up later in our treatment of the Exodus and of the Christ event. For the present we consider this other conclusion: it is not by deepening our theoretical study of the Scriptures or of the Christian faith that we will be able to recognize God in events. The opposite is the case. Because Christians have the grace—(which comes from the prophetic spirit bequeathed in baptism)—to discern God in their history, not only their individual history but also the history of their community and the world, they also have the gift of penetrating the unfathomable richness of God. To be attentive to history is to better understand the Gospel. A knowledge of the Scriptures, whether exhaustive or not, can be the basis for a science that explores the redactional or historical meaning of a text. But such an approach does not penetrate its reservoir-of-meaning which surpasses that level. Elsewhere we shall discuss in greater detail this hermeneutic assertion so often overlooked by exegetes.[9] The deepest Christian faith requires that both paths be tread: Christians must "read" the events in order to reformulate the traditional message; and they must hearken to the already transmitted word of God in order to be more open to the salvific events transpiring in the world. For a long time now we have tread only the latter path and have completely missed the manifestations of God in history, as he was manifested in an earlier time in the exodus event and so many others.

The God-of-history is a God-who-comes. He is not revealed only in the cosmos, but above all *in hope.* (The God of nature is always the same, as in the mythic worldviews, and does not challenge human freedom; instead this God deepens human consciousness of finitude, and perhaps of fate.) By revealing himself in history, God reveals to human beings the meaning of events and generates an interpersonal dialogue between God and human beings and among human beings. History emerges as "project." Human beings are fulfilled in their march forward and not in a cosmogonic cyclical recurrence. (Significantly there is no biblical or Christian feast of the New Year.)

Latin American liberation activity has a deep Christian meaning. As already noted, for Christians it is an ineluctable commitment. The peoples of the continent are discovering their vocation to freedom. Europe has not given this vocation; nor has the institutional Church done much to clarify it, because the Church was silenced—either by the powers that be or, what is even worse, by its own mentality, alienated by decrepit and consequently oppressive structures. It is from the new Christian grassroots communities that this marvelous re-discovery of the God-of-history surges up today. With growing pressure, this rediscovery is slowly affecting the hierarchical Church, the last to read the signs of the times. Such tardiness was, of course, sociologically predictable.

Specific mention must be made of the grassroots communities of Brazil, made up especially of poor and marginalized people. Their testimony is eloquent and their influence on the hierarchy is great. Also noteworthy is the hierarchy's capacity to attune itself to this testimony, adopting it as a new word of liberation or as a commitment of the episcopate itself.[10]

What happens when Christians deform the Gospel or can no longer read the presence of God in the events of the world? God cannot reveal himself in history, the events of which are weaving together the warp and the woof of his plan of salvation. There will always be those who "recognize" his step. Others will grasp it through a "de-struction," that is, by laying new foundations to an affirmation of God's presence—though the foundations seem to be negative. Such is the case with Marxism (as an accusation against Christianity for having perverted the message of justice and, consequently, of love) and of atheism (as the sign of the loss-of-meaning of the traditional representation of God).

Both contemporary phenomena are invested with the characteristics of the "signs of the times" for Christians capable of recognizing therein the true countenance of their God. Conservative Christians may be scandalized by atheists but the latter may be closer to God. Atheism is attributable to various motives. Perhaps the image of God has become superficial because of a self-sufficient and all-explaining science; but in this case Christians are relatively culpable because they were not prepared to understand the advent of science. Or perhaps the atheist is looking for the Absolute God or the author of history whose image has been disfigured. Consequently, the negation of the "god," who is not God, leads to a rediscovery of the authentic God, if not by atheists themselves, at least by Christians to the extent that they are challenged to re-encounter God and to re-express him. Even non-Christians discover God in a silent manner—the unknown God. And non-Christians unknowingly manifest God in their lifestyle, for example, in love of neighbor. I believe that the encounter of Christ with humankind—according to the eschatological scene of Matt. 25:31-46—is illuminating. It is only at the end that some realize that they *had known Christ*; others, who believed they had known him, are surprised to learn that in reality he was *in the brother.*

These reflections on the "signs of the times" have one intention within the framework of our undertaking to fashion a "hermeneutics of liberation": i.e., to assert that the Latin American liberation movements— with all their novelty and ambiguity—can be "read" from a Christian point of view as a manifestation of a new faith *commitment,* and an inescapable one at that. Moreover, if the liberation of our peoples is not grasped by the institutional Church (as in the case of Cuba) or occurs outside its ambit of expression (for example, the popular struggles) or is effected by independent groups, it is a sign that the Church is "asleep" in its interpretation of the Gospel and does not understand the situation of dependence and oppression of our peoples. Or it is a sign that the Church has strategically "introduced" the liberal and "pacifist" image that the oppressors, very "Christian" that they are, have helped to sustain and nourish. It is sad for the history of the Latin America Church, but such are the facts.[11] The many exceptions—and the good intentions—offer some consolation to our guilty consciences, but the reality is evident: the Church was long linked to the structures of dependence, and the great process of liberation that is growing in all Latin America is *not* an initiative of the Church. It is the great odyssey of *the oppressed people—* many of them grassroots Christians, of course—who began to sing the Vespers of a new Latin America and awakened the new Church, in gestation and committed to the cause of the oppressed.

To better understand this liberation process the pages that follow treat of the biblical message of liberation. But once more it must be stressed that we shall do so *from* the perspective of this Latin American process in which the reservoir-of-meaning of the kerygma of God's Word illumines us.

5. PLAN OF THE ANALYSIS

Our point of departure will be the liberation experience of the Exodus of the Hebrews from Egypt, as we try to deepen our understanding of its meaning. Strange as it may seem, it is only after reference to the Exodus that we can proceed to the book of Genesis (as we shall explain) and then re-encounter the God of the Covenant in the prophets. After considering these three moments of the Old Testament, we turn to two in the New: the "liberative" attitudes of Jesus (the Gospels) and the expression of the Paschal Mystery in "liberation" categories by St. Paul (Letter to the Romans). Our intention is to interrelate these kerygmatic "foci," to see their continuity, their mutual interpenetration, the successive "unfolding-of-meaning," the formation of a consciousness-of-freedom and a commitment to liberation as characteristic notes of Christian faith and praxis.

In accordance with our task, we wish to establish a hermeneutical perspective with a view to a "re-reading" of the biblical message of liberation *on the basis of* our experience as oppressed peoples or persons. It will be up to the readers to "situate" themselves vis-à-vis the Word of God, to explore its conscientizing and liberative meaning for themselves or in order to dialogue with their oppressed brothers and sisters. We do not wish here to make "applications" to the Latin American situation; this would be anti-hermeneutical because it would be tantamount to accommodating the biblical message to concrete cases. *My* hermeneutical moment is different from that of one or another reader. In order to write these pages from a hermeneutical and Latin American perspective, I do not first carry out an exegesis of the biblical passages and *subsequently* relate it to the facts of our world or our oppressed continent. Rather, the facts must be, and are, *prior* to my interpretation of the biblical Word. Only thus is my interpretation eisegetical (literally, "that which leads *in*") and not purely exegetical ("that which leads *out*"). Readers will be able to orientate themselves in the interpretation of the sacred message on the basis of this hermeneutical effort, but they will have to "say their own word" in extension of mine and confront the Word from *their* own situation. Even when there is a common lived experience, continental in a certain sense, each of us has an inner world of our own and our social experience. It is essential that the readers read themselves in the Word of the kerygma and that they tell it to others and practice it, that is, convert it to *praxis*. The readers' own word—which becomes a new hermeneutics in a chain-like succession—is more important than mine. And all will see that *their* own "word-praxis" will surge up more spontaneously than they might have at first believed. Here I am referring especially to the dialogical word, to the communitarian group: or community-based hermeneutics of the biblical message. Anyone who has had the least experience of grassroots communities knows the richness and depth of the people in understanding the kerygma.

CHAPTER II

Exodus: Event and Word

1. THE EXODUS AS "RESERVOIR-OF-MEANING"

We take for granted here that the reader is familiar with the biblical account of the Exodus, which comes between the patriarchal narratives (epoch of the Promise) and the entry into Canaan (epoch of the fulfillment of the Promise). The experience of Egypt is a *tension* (the "God of the Father" has forgotten his people) and a *dis-tension* (Yahweh remembers his Promise, cf. Exod. 6:4-5!). The vicissitudes of the passage through the desert form a thematic and significative unity with the departure from Egypt.[1] Accordingly the present reflections comprise the data contained in the books of Exodus, Numbers, and the homiletic "memorial" of the first part of Deuteronomy (1-11). At any rate, we shall concentrate on the first chapters (1-15) of Exodus.

Many biblical scholars or theologians have already explored the Exodus event in depth in relation to the new journey of Latin America's "liberation."[2] It is a characteristic, provocative, creative, inexhaustible kerygmatic "locus." It is an exemplary passage, more specifically relevant to a theology of liberation than to a theology freedom. And this is why it is explored more in a Latin American than in a European theological context.

We do not wish to treat of the Exodus because it is voguish, nor in order to repeat what has already been elaborated. Our intention is to fathom other possibilities of the Word of the Exodus and to sketch their hermeneutical perspectives. This should enable the readers—viewed as a collective audience more than as individuals—to "say their word."

Let us begin by situating the Exodus account within the totality of the Old Testament and its meaning within the complex of the biblical worldview. In both cases the Exodus is the key event that models the faith of Israel. Unless we begin from this central event, neither Israel's faith nor the formation of its religious traditions and sacred books are understandable. The more Israel becomes engaged in forming itself as a people, the more it focuses on that *decisive* event, which—therefore—is represented in a creational language (see especially Deutero-Isaiah: 44:21-24; 51:9-11, the allusion to creation as a struggle against the forces of chaos; 54:5, Deut. 32:6; etc.).

Cosmogony exercises a dramatic fascination in all religions. It is the epiphany of being, the moment in which sacredness penetrates the cosmos; it is the plenitude of the new, of that which is not exhausted by the corrosive time of finitude and of death. As important as origins are, the Hebrew worldview shifts them to another epicenter, the salvific event of the Exodus. History displaces the cosmic. God is visualized in human events more than in the phenomena of the physical world. But the Exodus as a historical and salvific happening is so "originary" that it attracts to itself the creational experience as expressed in the mythically structured language of the biblical account.

For us this means that the Exodus is established as a *radical* datum, exceedingly profound, *in which* both Israel and we ourselves must interpret God and ourselves. The Exodus becomes an inexhaustible "reservoir-of-meaning." For this reason its "donation-of-meaning" is unlimited, whence its unique hermeneutical possibilities for Latin American theology. These assertions will be clarified in what follows.

2. FROM THE EVENT TO THE WORD

It would be useful to provide a hermeneutical key here now: all human experience engenders its "word." In what manner? Insofar as its "significance" emerges as the key-event occasions other lived experiences or situations, or as we begin to interpret ourselves in the light of that event, which, as a result, begins to appear ever more *radical* and more laden with significance. In the "afterward" of its own facticity it is grasped as *foundational* of the present.

An event is not viewed as decisive in the history of a person or of a people at the moment it occurs but only *after* the mediation that time effects, after it has "donated" its recreative energy. Our personal experience is full of these disclosures-of-meaning of events that emerge only much later, or by degrees, from their originally hidden depths. The same thing happens in the history of peoples. In the first years of the independence of the peoples of Latin America the liberating actions did not have—on a conscious level—the same importance that they began to acquire in the subsequent "memorial."

Furthermore, *today,* they appear to us with dimensions that they did not have a half century ago. Our forebears perhaps celebrated them with the merriment of independence gained. But—as a result of a new concientization—we recognize that we are not independent but have merely changed masters. For that reason our patriotic festivals are converted into "programmatic" and vocational celebrations for Latin Americans. In other words they appear to us in another dimension, a dimension that is deeper because it points up our historical "project" in a more radical way by reminding us of what we must be and not yet are. Therefore they are celebrations in hope because they announce more than what they have been up to now. They are not remembered "in tranquility" but prophetically.

Accordingly we understand the salvific Exodus event as the Hebrews themselves did, namely, hermeneutically, either by "exploring" its meaning from the perspective of new situations that completed the Exodus (for example, the victories over the Transjordanian kings who would not permit them access to the Promised Land, cf. Num. 21:10-35; Ps. 135:10-12, etc.), or by measuring the magnitude of the liberation by what they subsequently became as a free people on their own land. For the Hebrews the Exodus always signified the ontological origin of their present reality, or it became a challenging "memory" when they ceased to be free.

Where and when do we find testimony of this re-signification of the Exodus? How did it become more "intentioning" for later generations of Hebrews than for their forebears who had lived through it? We reply: the unfolding of the latent meaning of the first Exodus occurred in the lineal prolongation of that liberation and was expressed in a "word." This word was "recharged" with fresh meanings by successive hermeneutical re-readings up to the time it was fixed permanently as expressing a whole worldview in the Exodus *account* in its present form. The Exodus is thus not the bald happening that took place around the thirteenth century B.C., but rather represents the event as it was reflected upon, pondered, and explored by faith and grasped in all its projections. This explains why the narration of the book of Exodus "says" much more than what actually transpired at that time.

For this reason it is *message*. The profundity does not consist in the historical phenomenon as it might be photographed or registered in a chronicle, but in its significance, which can be understood only at a distance and which is "said" in the word. This happens with any experience of a decisive character, as we have said. When we tell about an event that was significant for our own lives, we put ourselves at a distance from its past exteriority and we inject into it the self-understanding that is now ours *since and because* of that event.

But when the event is contemplated from within the perspective of faith and the manifestation of God is recognized in it, the word-account that "re-signifies" it is interpreted as the Word of God. And as such it enters into a rotating process through which it is always "memory" and it is always "announcement." At the same time that it is incorporating its own new manifestations, through its re-reading (or re-writing!), it is also challenging as Word open to a new historical expression. The past becomes "promise" for those who hearken to this Word.

We are not saying this to set forth a theory or for intellectual satisfaction, the pleasure of discovering something. Rather, all this suggests that the Exodus is an event fraught with meaning, as indicated by the biblical account and the experience of Israel, and that it is still *unconcluded*. If our reading of the biblical kerygma means anything, the "memory" of the Exodus becomes a provocative Word, an announcement of liberation for us, the oppressed peoples of the Third World. We are enjoined to prolong the Exodus event because it was not an event solely for the Hebrews but rather the manifestation of a liberative plan of God for all peoples. According to a hermeneutical line of thinking it is perfectly possible that we might understand ourselves *from* the perspective or the biblical Exodus and, above all, that we might understand the Exodus *from* the vantage point of our situation as peoples in economic, political, social, or cultural "bondage."

3. FROM THE EVENT TO THE PROMISE

We have already said that the reading of the Exodus account—as an existential "re-reading"—becomes a "promise" *for us*. The theme of the promise expresses the consciousness of an unfinished historical project and, at the same time, confidence that it will be implemented. Thus it is the backward projection of a hope straining toward the future. We spoke of the hermeneutical circle, through which the event becomes Word-meaning and this Word-meaning "announces" a new expression of the event. This same circle is also apparent in the opposite direction of the event projected backwards. Thus the salvific event, once profoundly understood, is seen as *plan,* that is, as something that was prepared before it occurred.

In a mythical worldview, the event can be explained as fate, but in a theological conception of the world (oriented to a goal) this anticipation is expressed in the language of the Promise. The Promise is not historically prior to the event, just as the Word-account was not contemporary to it. Rather, it follows the event and becomes a new form of "radicalization" in its *meaning*. The deeper the meaning, the more inclusive it is. The more significance the Exodus event accumulates, the more it appears as having been laid out beforehand in God's plans. If a person has had a function of capital importance for the consciousness of a people, that person is represented as having been "called" from before birth (Jeremiah, the Servant of Yahweh, Christ, and later Paul were "commissioned" or elected while still in the maternal womb or even before: Jer. 1:4f.; Isa. 49:1, 5; Luke 1:26ff.; Gal. 1:15). It is important to understand that these narratives are *posterior* to the function discharged by such personages. The value of what is "originary" (like the importance of creation) is projected into the historical. Such is the case with the Exodus. The event retrospectively becomes "promise" in two ways: first, in the account of the vocation of Moses (Exod. 3, 6) and in the announcement of liberation; second, in the accounts of the archetypical Promise addressed to Abraham and his two descendants, Isaac and Jacob (Gen. 12:1ff., etc.). The latter promise is conceived in the clear terms of "land" (as nation) and of descent (as people); and Israel became a nation and people only *after and through* the Exodus, a long time after Abraham.

We do not deny that there could have been a vocation experienced as such by the patriarchs or a call to the Hebrew slaves in Egypt, but the Promise, or the vocation, *as narrated,* takes for granted the experience of the liberation and the existence of Israel as a people on its land. The Promise expresses in the form of a plan the event which, in reality, engenders the Promise as word. Such is the richness of the Promise, or of the language of "vocation." It speaks with a depth not grasped at the time of Abraham and of Moses. Are not we ourselves using a similar language when we assert or discover a "historical vocation" in the Latin American peoples? Why do we voice it *now,* or when this vocation *is being* implemented, instead of holding it to have been known before? Simply because the language of vocation (or promise, in a religious context and expressed in religious language) is a manner of "saying" the deepest sense of an event, *from* the perspective of the event itself.

We conclude, therefore, that the Exodus is the programmatic event of the religious experience of Israel that establishes the value of the Word-account and of the Promise. We have emphasized it because of its hermeneutical implications. We shall examine the content of the account under five headings: the situation of the Hebrews in Egypt, the word-response (of the oppressed, of the liberator, and finally of the oppressor), the event itself and its episodes, the hermeneutical "account" (in mythico-symbolic language), and the message of this narrative.

4. ANALYSIS OF THE SITUATION

Hebrew tribes had infiltrated the fertile zone of the Nile delta in northern Egypt, driven perhaps by a wave of migrations of Semitic groups originating in Syria; the hieroglyphic annals call them "Hyksos." This movement began in the eighteenth century B.C. and continued up to at least the sixteenth. This hypothesis is very schematic and shrouds many problems, such as the "gap" of some centuries between the epoch of the patriarchs and the generation of the Exodus in the eighteenth century. Our only concern here is to call attention to historical events lived by small, scientifically established human groups; these are the originators of the "discovery" of a *presence* of God.

The slavery of the Israelites in the country of the Nile took its concrete features from the customs of that time. Ramses II and other pharaohs used prisoners, slaves, and marginalized or recently arrived and unstable peoples to build great cities. The biblical account itself confirms this: "Therefore they set taskmasters over them to afflict them with heavy burdens; and they built for Pharaoh store-cities, Pithom and Rameses" (1:11). The Bible describes these episodes as an "oppression" (cf. v. 12, and section 5a below). This was a form of slavery not only because the Israelites "belonged" to a lord (as in pagan antiquity and in many regions of the modern world, for example, Saudi Arabia or Brazil). It was also oppressive, forced labor. It was an alienating situation in the extreme like, in our time, the shameful situation of the Puerto Ricans exploited at all levels by their masters.[3] All exploitation is characterized by an ignominious, arrogant arbitrariness, whether it is exercised by a pharaoh or by the imperialist countries of our own day.

How could they not cry out in such a situation? What good is this impotent anguish? The alienation of the Hebrews reaches such a limit that they are *incapable of hoping for salvation:* "Moses spoke thus to the people of Israel; but they *did not listen* to Moses, *because of their broken spirit* and their cruel bondage" (Exod. 6:9). This is not "infidelity" to grace but a total human estrangement that annuls even hope, the last possibility of liberation. Perhaps this sentence—unique in the entire Bible—has not been given its due attention in the many readings that we may have made of this chapter. But it stands out in all its crushing violence when we "rediscover" it in so many concrete cases of oppressed people; we need go no farther than the marginalized Argentineans in the provinces, the Creoles, the exploited workers who never have an opportunity to fulfill themselves as human beings endowed with dignity and equal to others.

This is what Paulo Freire makes so clear when he asserts that the oppressed internalize the oppressors—and consequently their own situation as oppressed people—in such a way that they cannot imagine any other possibility nor any change whatsoever that might "liberate" them.[4] Far from being a secondary datum, the assertion in Exodus 6:9 signals, in letters of fire, the summit of human alienation when people no longer even hope in their own liberation. This situation is even worse when it is "internalized" through an interpretation of the sacred, as in the case of the Indians of Guatamala who celebrate Holy Week without the Resurrection. They thereby internalize their own "crushed identity,"[5] which they must accommodate to that of a falsified Christ. This is not due to any fault of theirs, to be sure, but to a sad hermeneutical process whose point of departure is their situation as an oppressed people.

The alienated subjects not only have no consciousness of what they can "be" or do, but they also accept that things could not be otherwise. They can even believe that their condition is good, if not the best. This does not apply, of course, to socio-economic alienation but to its religious counterpart, which we shall analyze later. Before "conscientization" the alienated subjects accept the reality that they live as their natural condition. The conscientization occurs through "word," discussed in the following section, or through events. The Exodus *event* will engender the *consciousness-of-freedom* of the people of Israel, which will be further deepened in the subsequent word, as we have seen. Judging from biblical references it would appear that the Israelites had not "internalized" the state of oppression as the condition proper to them. Indeed, the Israelites "groan" and "cry" before Yahweh, their God (Exod. 3:7, 9; 6:5). Let us recall nevertheless that this account is an "interpretation" of the event. Its purpose is to dramatize the "presence" of the liberator God. The unexpected "novelty" of the manifestation of Yahweh to Moses (Exod. 3:6ff.), indicates that the people were far from knowing anything about any ancient "promise" or a presence of its God in history. Indeed, the passage cited (6:9) describes a hopeless prostration. Nevertheless, a "conscientization" through the word or through events is always possible.

The biblical account of the Exodus is illuminating even in this respect.

Before passing on to the next theme another assessment of the state of the oppressed people is called for. Their situation is of a political and social order. The oppression in Egypt is of a *political* order because it is the authority of the pharaoh that exploits a group in his country, an alien ethnic minority to boot. The oppression is exercised from the seat of political power. It was also a way of getting rid of the hated Asiatics, as we know from the Egyptian texts. The charge of genocide is accurate. Not only did the forced labor projects wipe out multitudes; there was also the additional intention to exterminate the race through infanticide—equivalent to the genocidal "sterilization" that is practiced in Latin America under the euphemism of "family planning' orchestrated by the North Americans.[6] The Hebrews, in fact, were numerous, and this constituted a political danger for the internal security of the kingdom (Exod. 1:7, 9: "Come, let us deal shrewdly with them, lest they multiply, and, if war befall us, they join our enemies and fight against us and escape from the land."). Accordingly the Egyptians put oppressive taskmasters over them (v.11) and ordered the midwives to kill the male children (vv. 15ff.).

If such is the case, the liberation of the Israelites in Egypt was an event of *political* and *social* implications. God did not begin saving in the spiritual order, not even from *sin*. God saves total human beings whose *human* fulfillment can be impeded not only by themselves (sin) but also by other human beings who abuse their power or their social status. This observation has grave hermeneutical consequences for a Latin American or Third World rereading of the message of the Exodus event. Have we paid sufficient attention to the fact that the first, exemplary liberation event, which "reveals" the God of salvation, was political and social? We shall take up this point again when we discuss the New Testament.

5. THE WORD THAT PRECEDES LIBERATION

We have the "situation." There is also a "word" of the oppressed, of the liberating God, and of the oppressor. What function and value does each have?

a. The word of the oppressed people. The two accounts of the vocation of Moses contain the voice of the oppressed human being expressed indirectly in Yahweh's own words: "I have seen the *affliction* of my people who are in Egypt, and have heard their *cry* because of their taskmasters . . ." (3:7); "and now behold, the cry of the people of Israel has come to me . . ." (3:9). And in the later, priestly account (6:1–13): "Moreover I have heard the *groaning* of the people of Israel whom the Egyptians hold in bondage . . ." (6:5).

The word of the oppressed is the "cry." It is a mere passive lamentation, an expression of sorrow? Would it not rather be to move God, signifying that they hope for salvation only from him?

The "cry" theme is illustrated in various Mesopotamian myths, the most outstanding of which is the *Atrahasis*. It is a poem, written about 2000 B.C., on the human condition (with a tradition of the Flood different from that found in the epic of Gilgamesh). It is a *social* myth. A first scene recounts the rebellion of the minor gods, who work, against the three masters Anu, Enlil, and Enki, who govern the world without working and who live on the fruits of the minor gods' labor. The rebellion, which takes the form of a "strike" and includes an attack on Enlil's palace (symbol of power and tyranny), is crowned with success. The threat hanging over the higher gods prompts them to devise a solution: *the creation of human beings to do all the work,* thus ensuring a permanent leisure also to the minor gods. The latter are liberated, but at the expense of another oppressed being, the humans.

In the Babylonian creation epic (*Enuma Elish*) the fate of humankind is likewise to toil for the gods. And this fate seems to be accepted in a kind of "closed consciousness," in which the image of the world is as it has always been conceptualized and inherited. The myth of Atrahasis, on the other hand, presents the figure of more conscientized human beings, who, moreover, as they multiply also rebel (like the toiling deities who preceded them). The unity of many is a prerequisite for a successful rebellion against an unacceptable order (Exod. 1:9f.). The oppressors perforce must reduce their number—not destroy them, at least at first, if they want to remain as masters—in order to prevent their ascendance. So the god Enlil, the taskmaster of the work-projects (construction of dikes and canals, typical of the tasks performed on Mesopotamian soil) tries to decimate humankind, first through pestilence, then by drought, and finally—now enraged by the intervention of another god, friendly to humankind, Enki (a parallel to the Hesiodic and tragic Prometheus)—by flood. But he is foiled once more since Atrahasis, the "very intelligent" protagonist (that is what his name means) saves himself thanks to help from Enki himself, and thus humankind perdures on earth. Furious, Enlil persists in his evil designs and afflicts women with *sterility* and other genetic deficiencies, the objective still being the numerical reduction of "dangerous" humankind.

There is a tragic quality in this extraordinary myth, since humankind fails in its efforts at self-liberation. This is not said just to point out again that history repeats itself. But at least the myth announces the feat of rebellion, which even has its archetype in that of the minor gods. This uprising is anticipated with the word "cry" (*rigmu* in Babylonian),[7] which brings to mind the cry of the Hebrews in the passages cited above. On the one hand, the situation in the Mesopotamian myth seems more authentic: humankind rebels and *struggles*; the "cry" of the children of Israel, instead, seems more passive. They cry out to their God instead of acting. On the other hand, the Mesopotamian worldview does not allow a liberating escape for oppressed human beings since there is no hermeneutical and conscientizing event like the Exodus. The myth culminates with human frustration. Moreover, as an account of an archetypical "event," it retro-spectively injects that frustration into the account: the *desire* for liberation remains truncated.

The Hebrews "cry out" to Yahweh, while they "hope" for liberation.

The deep religious sense of the biblical worldview emphasizes the *divine* initiative of the process, but this is peculiar to religious *language*; it does not mean that this is the way it occurred historically. It is opportune to point this out, since some theologians who intepret the Bible literally delight in disproving the authenticity of "human" initiatives of liberation. They ignore the fact that the Exodus could have been, from an initial perspective, an intention that arose from among the Hebrews themselves. It was the "event" that, from its very core, was manifesting a divine *presence* with all its implications (including the Covenant). This assertion is pertinent today, since there are liberation processes in our world that seem disconnected from the Gospel, but which, little by little, assume a configuration bespeaking a presence of Christ the liberator. Examples are the peoples and groups struggling to change the situation of oppression on our continent. Here a hermeneutical implication is again apparent.

Summing up, the biblical datum of the "cry" of the Hebrews, passive at first sight, has struck us as richly suggestive. This datum points out, moreover, that people begin to be conscientized—and to embark on the path to liberation—when they implore, raise their voices, their shouts of protest and denunciation. Such is the word of the oppressed in the Exodus account.

b. The word of the liberator. In the two vocational accounts of Exodus 3 and 6, Yahweh is represented as one who knows of the oppression of the people of Israel ("I have seen, . . . I have heard," 3:7-9; 6:5) as the revealer of a plan of immediate salvation ("I have come down to deliver them," 3:8; "I will bring you out from under the burdens . . . ," 6:6ff.), which culminates in the gift of the land (3:8; 6:4-8) and in the establishment of a free nation (6:7). As is proper to his mode of acting, Yahweh chooses an intermediary as leader, in this case Moses. By expressing this divine plan, people of faith profess a consciousness of their own vocation to freedom in a transcendent sense. Hence it is an unrenounceable vocation. To deny it is to efface one's own countenance, to lose one's being. So significant is this vocation, expressed as the "plan" of God, that the very name of God utters it.

Exodus 3 describes a humble visual theophany transformed into a spectacular theo-*logy*, or epiphany of the Word, in which God reveals his name of Yahweh, "he-who-makes-(Israel)-exist," the liberator who re-creates his destroyed people. God makes known his dynamic name, a name that remains marked by the memory of the Exodus, in the context of the liberation from the bondage of Egypt. Only much later, when a metaphysical expression of God is given, will Yahweh be interpreted as "he that is"; the idols are "nothing." This conception, notable in Deutero-Isaiah (40:18ff. etc.), will be consecrated in the Greek version of the Bible ("I am who I am"). But, originally Yahweh is the name of the "Lord of Hosts," of the holy war. It is a programmatic name, bearing a plan from on high and generating hope. "Yahweh" is the characteristic name of God of the Hebrews; their cult and their faith remained focused on the remembrance and the invocation of the "Liberator" God.

The word of God also has a conscientizing function: first, through the revelation of a salvific plan, expressed here in clear terms of liberation; second, through the dialogue with Moses, the leader of the people who interprets that plan in the form of a vocation to lead the process. Moses' understanding of his new commitment comes slowly, as is apparent from the fivefold objection he makes: "Who am I that I should go to Pharaoh?" (Exod. 3:11); "If I come to the people . . . and they ask me . . ." (3:13); ". . . they will not believe me . . ." (4:1); "Oh, my Lord, I am not eloquent . . ." (4:10); ". . . send, I pray some other person" (4:13). The doubts and the refusals of the leader can be explained in terms *of Moses himself,* because he knows that the mission entrusted to him is difficult. But they also reflect the doubts *of the people,* sunk in prostration and devoid of hope. Therefore the intention of the account of the dialogue between Yahweh and Moses is to "melt" the heart of the people so that it may begin the liberating process. It must be noted that only in this Yahwist-Elohist account of Exodus 3–5 do the people come to "believe" (cf. 4:31); the reason is that the clarifying word, which convinces from within, was given.

The oppressors are the only ones who cannot be conscientized. We know, moreover, that the oppressors never liberate either others or themselves. On the contrary, when a liberation process affecting them comes into being they hermetically withdraw and oppress with even greater violence. This is what happens in the Exodus account: the pharaoh "hardens" (a felicitous word to indicate the psychology of the oppressor!). The lengthy account of the plagues (7–11) depicts the crescendo of the egoism of pharaonic power. But that is not all: the oppressor hardens not only in his innermost being by not accepting change and by opposing the freedom of the oppressed, but also *by oppressing even more.* Upon learning of the liberation plan (Exod. 5:1–5) he exploits them to the maximum, demanding of them the same daily quota of bricks with the added obligation of finding the straw for making the bricks by themselves (5:6–19). The history of slavery and of oppression is replete with pages like this. What is happening, for example, in the Brazilian Amazon and in various other countries is but the recrudescence of an old system.[8]

The upshot of this inhuman method is obvious: the intimidation of the oppressed. But this fear by itself would not be of great moment if it were merely external, while the root decision to be free were actually being strengthened, as so frequently occurs. The grave danger is that it begets an inner fear, "the fear of freedom," the fear of taking up freedom with all its risks.[9] Ultimately, it means siding with the oppressor and opposing the liberator. Exodus 5:20ff. illustrates this phenomenon. After the "hardening" of the pharaoh, who has been informed of the subversive plan, and after the imposition of the new daily work assignments, the people's representatives to the palace upbraid Moses and Aaron with these accusations: ". . . you have made us offensive in the sight of Pharaoh and his servants, and have put a sword in their hand to kill us." In a certain way they are siding with the king, preferring that things continue as they are. The "cause" of the evil is not in the pharaoh but in those who conscientize and promote the cause of freedom. But that is not all. Moses also "internalizes" this fear of freedom and passes on the accusation to God himself, the ultimate author of the liberation plan: "O Lord, why hast thou *done evil* to this people? Why didst thou ever *send* me? For since I came to Pharaoh *to speak* in thy name, he has done evil to this people, *and thou hast not delivered thy people*" (Exod. 5:22ff.). It is as though the itinerary descending from the conscientizing Word were inverted by a word ascending from the oppressor or from his "shadow."

c. *The word of the oppressor.* We have already commented on this theme in part. It is his "hardening" in egoism and his blindness in the face of the reality of the others. The account of the plagues points up a notable attitude of the Egyptian oppressor: his heart "hardens" when Yahweh warns him through punishments (a "religious" form of subversive action) and also when Yahweh forgives him and lets him act *from within himself:* on that occasion he reveals his oppressive soul (cf. 8:11, 27f.; 9:34f.; 10:20). No word of God (his conscience) nor of the oppressed manages to move him. He cannot provide any solution from within himself. The oppressor can never free. The pharaoh's replies to the messengers of the divine plan—Moses and Aaron—are rejections, or cunning tricks (as in the case of 10:11 in which he authorizes only the men to leave, thus forcing them to return to their families) or lies. The oppression serves his interests or aggrandizes his *power.* Yahweh's opposition in the form of his prodigies—through Aaron's feats with the rod—arouses his own will to power.

This confrontation of "powers" is significant since it prepares the great moment of liberation as an act of God's *force.* The Hebrews have no power whatsoever, being in a state of servitude and stripped of any means to effect their liberation. Only a superior power can help them, thus the manifestation of the plagues and Yahweh's salvific intervention in behalf of his people.

We stress once more that the account is essentially religious and that, therefore, the initiative and the guarantees, or the power, of liberation are attributed to God. It would be ingenuous to hope that the same will happen today, in a literal form. That immediate "presence" of God is more representational than literal. I mean to say that it did not manifest itself exactly in *that* way, but it was "recognized" from the perspective of the event itself and subsequently expressed in the mythico-symbolic language that we now read in the book of Exodus. We now know the richness that this phenomenon of "deepening" reveals.

Now we want to comment on the manifestation of the *power* of Yahweh, superior to that of the oppressor pharaoh, who can be overcome only by another "power." Now today there is a very clear consciousness that there is no power superior to that of a united and committed "people." When an entire people rejects a tyrant it creates an irremissible "power vacuum." The Hebrews' decision to rebel *collectively* and to flee (it was not a question of seizing power!) ensured their success. The pharaoh could do nothing against a united group. But this group was organized and did not hesitate to march because it had been "conscientized" and knew what it had to do, despite the initial resistance and doubt. The religious focus of the account does not provide us with the elements to judge the "strategy" of the liberation epic, but it does tell us that a liberation process having all the contours of a political and social event can very well be interpreted—indeed should be interpreted for a Christian conscience—as the will of God.

6. THE EVENT OF LIBERATION

What we have considered thus far in the biblical account is the preparation for and the becoming conscious of a vocation to freedom. The liberation event itself unfolds in various episodes that shall now be the subject of our reflections.

a. The Passover. The whole of chapter 12 of Exodus sets forth the ritual of the Passover interpreted as a "memorial" of the salvific event (vv. 14, 17, 27, 42, 51). The origin of a rite that was in the process of formation over a period of many years is clearly being ascribed to that particular moment. Moreover, the development occurred long after the event described. But this itself is significant for once again we have a case of an "unfolding-of-meaning" of that saving event. Each "passover" recalled this *presence* of God in the history of the people (in fact, all Jewish feasts were being referred to the Exodus). Thus all later significant events were understood in the light of the originary liberation, the passover, by commemorating that first event, including all its consequences. It should be pointed out that, since the Passover is a typical religious phenomenon, what transpired in the Paschal "memory" down through the centuries was understood to have been realized *in the first* Passover.

Every hermeneutical circle runs in two directions: from the archetypical event to the existential present and vice-versa, simultaneously assimilating all the intermediate moments, which are not added like links to the last "rereading" but which, rather, are fused with it. I can celebrate the Passover only because the Exodus event occurred, but in this "memory" I also recall the other moments of the people's liberation. Even the "Passover" of Christ is a continuation of the Exodus. But any "memory" has meaning for me only if I am in some way involved in a *present-day* process of liberation. Oppressors cannot celebrate the Passover; it would be a falsehood. At most, they might be able to re-adapt some pharaonic festivity. The Passover is of no use to them; it is a "subversive memory."

b. The departure from Egypt. The liberation event itself is related in Exodus 12–15. We are all familiar with the episodes of the departure from the land of the pharaohs. We should like merely to note two details: on the one hand the king "lets up" when he feels the noose around his neck (the death of the first-born, 12:29–33). Even so, his decision is forced. His consciousness continues to be that of an oppressor who cannot free anyone on his own initiative, from within himself. In fact, he does not feel right *without* the oppressed. The vertigo of power overtakes him and he exclaims: "What is this we have done, that we have let Israel go *from serving us?*" (14:5). Whereupon he sets out in hot pursuit in order to "retain" them as slaves. He needs them as the lord and master that he is. Without them, he no longer "is." Without their services, he is not the great pharaoh of Egypt. He ceases to be an oppressor only when the Hebrews save themselves *from him*. But at that same moment he destroys himself and all the trappings and entourage of his power (14:28).

Something noteworthy also transpires in the hearts of the Hebrews, in the culminating stage of their liberative process. Despite all the guarantees (symbolized in the word and in the guiding hand of God, and in his presence through the cloud and fire), the people yield to a last "doubt" when the danger is extreme and it seems as everything will come to naught (14:9f.). They "murmur" against their leader: "Is it because there are no graves in Egypt that you have taken us away to die in the wilderness? What have you done to us, in bringing us out of Egypt? Is not this what we said to you in Egypt, 'Let us alone and let us *serve* the Egyptians?' For it would have been better for us to serve the Egyptians than to *die* in the wilderness" (14:11ff.). Paradoxical as it may seem, the episode is deeply meaningful: the "conscientization" prior to a liberation process, and which sets it in motion, is never complete. *Only the event itself* reveals all its "meaning." The example of the Exodus is significant in this respect as well. And this is why the redactor underscores the conclusion: the sense of security that comes *from the event:* "And Israel saw the great work which the Lord did against the Egyptians, and the people feared the Lord; and they *believed* in the Lord and in his servant Moses" (14:31).

c. *The triumphal song*. The "meaning" arises from the event. This is what we have been asserting all along as the central theme of this essay. Praise is a way of expressing meaning. It is "interpretation." As such, it says something more than what actually happened. The thanksgiving prayer is different from the earlier petition; it is deeper. One petitions according to the "wish," which at times is illusion. But one shows gratitude according to the event, and the event is immediately revealed as "donor-of-meaning" through prolongations in the present life. And the event, because it corrects the wish, paradoxically appears as even more profound than the wish. The evocation of the saving God is deeper if it was preceded by the invocation. But the evocation, not the invocation, is hermeneutical. The magnificent "song of the Sea" (Exod. 15) evokes Yahweh as the agent of liberation:

> I will sing to the Lord,
> for he has triumphed gloriously;
> the horse and his rider
> he has thrown into the sea.
> The Lord is my strength and my song,

and he has become my salvation;
this is my God, and I will praise him,
my father's God, and I will exalt him.
The Lord is a man of war;
the Lord is his name (Exod. 15:1-4).

In this praise, however, we note the same phenomenon that we observed in the passover ritual (Exod. 12:1ff.): its redaction, as we know it, came much after the original event. It takes for granted, among other things, Israel's installation in the land of Canaan, a mountainous country that in verse 17 is represented as the "sanctuary" fashioned by the hands of Yahweh. In other words, the Exodus event is interpreted from the vantage point of the fulfillment in the promised land: the two moments of the "departure" (from Egypt) and of the "entry" (into the promised land) are correlates. The former points to the latter; the entry not only completes the departure but it also deepens its meaning, which was not totally perceptible at the moment of the liberation itself. Freedom was the goal of liberation, but it also gave liberation a new meaning. The "song of the sea" of Exodus 15 celebrates the God of the Exodus at the very moment of the liberation (cf. v. 1), but *from* the perspective of the full gift of the land; it also includes in the praise a broad, accumulated experience of salvation understood as a continuation of the originary exodus event. What can singing a Te Deum on the occasion of a patriotic feast "signify" for us *today*?

7. THE HERMENEUTICAL ACCOUNT

Up to now our reflections have been on the "event" level. Nevertheless we have throughout taken for granted the account in the book of Exodus as we know it today. The event itself and its narration, however, are not fully consonant with one another (see Sec. 2 of this chapter). We can now restrict ourselves to the word-account, briefly alluded to already. The narration says *more* than what outwardly occurred in the action of liberation. It is "interpretation" that never distorts the event but that, instead, enriches it with a deeper vision.

The language of our account has a symbolic and mythical structure. The *event* is not mythical, for it has nothing to do with the primordial history of the gods (the "intention" of which, on the other hand, does not cease to be "truthful"). Rather, the event has to do with the historical experience of slavery and salvation that the Hebrews had known in Egypt. Nevertheless, when an event is interpreted in its transcendent meaning, it cannot be narrated simply as chronicle or in its external reality. Through a characteristic process, analyzed phenomenologically, the level of transcendence "passes" into the contingent exteriority of the event, which suddenly includes "miraculous" and extraordinary elements. The peculiarity of mythico-symbolic narration is that it is fundamentally *hermeneutical*. More exactly, *because* it is hermeneutical (that is, it deciphers the event), it requires a language different from that of secular historiography.

Thus the symbol refers us to the transcendent order, and the myth refers to the archetypical and creational order. This is the source of the typical religious language, which is not absent from the Bible (nor can it be), that constantly speaks of a presence of God in human events. Biblical history discovers "meaning" more than it reproduces contingent facts. The account of the liberation in Exodus 1–15 is replete with symbolic images and mythical events (plagues, the fabulous passage of the sea, God's dialogues with Moses, the drowning of the pharaoh with his hosts, the pillar of smoke or of fire, etc.). We repeat for the non-initiated in the study of religious language that it is not a matter of historical distortion but of an exploration of the transcendent meaning of things or events. A "sacred history" cannot be identical in form with an ordinary chronicle of the same event. But they are not two parallel histories. Sacred history probes the plan and the significance of known human history. The perspective and the language are different, and it is more profound that they should be so. Hence there is no ground for wonderment if we find this eminently appropriate language in the account of the liberation of the people of Israel.

This phenomenon also occurs in our own history. Despite the scientific and historicist mentality in which we, as Westerners, have been living for centuries, accounts of patriotic feats are handed down to us along with not a few modifications. The "heroes" may be such from the very beginning. At other times they are "comprehended" in this category much later, because of what they *signified*. And at still other times, some, who were not so important at first or for a particular group, move into the foreground. A "historical revisionism" is justified when it denounces the utilization of patriotic figures for ends diametrically opposed to those of the original liberating revolution or the obscuring of others who are not "serviceable" to the spurious interests of a new caste of oppressors.

A well-informed person knows that there are national "heroes" who have rendered no great service to the country, others who have been kept "under wraps," and still others upon whom an "erasio memoriae" has been perpetrated. But "revisionism" fails when it presumes to lay bare the mythic elements that have grown around the founding patriotic figures. In the mythic account the people make "explicit" the *meaning* of this or that personage for the *whole* of a specific history, its meta-event dimension. Likewise, the Hebrews were not content with the unadorned data on Moses in the Exodus account—even though the leader of the liberation had *already* been mythologized. So they enlarged his figure with innumerable apocryphal episodes, each more extraordinary than the last. This is not to be viewed as an eagerness to indulge in fabulation but as a hermeneutical expression of a profound understanding of the key-personage of their history.

8. THE MESSAGE

What we have expounded so far repeatedly points up the kerygmatic richness of the Exodus account. To conclude, we shall comment on four other aspects of this message, each time leaving a line of reflection for the reader to pursue.

a. Salvation-liberation. The Exodus was the salvific experience of Israel. This meant that this people deepened and expanded its understanding of salvation, the fundamental component of any religious worldview, in terms of liberation. The Hebrew words *nasal* and *yasa* connote the two aspects by turns. It happened also that the particular history of this people—without any post-mortem eschatology or body-soul dualism—emphasized an experience of God as savior on the terrestrial plane; salvation was closely related to the political and the social spheres in which "independence" was a concrete and existential expression of the protection of its God. This has consequences for a theology of history: God is understood as *savior* because he acts *in human history,* and not, in the first place, in a meta-history.

In the faith of Israel, professed in the central creeds (e.g., Deut. 6:20ff.; 26:5ff.; Josh. 24:2-13; etc.), "salvation" is equivalent to "liberation" and God is defined *in terms of the Exodus,* that is, as "liberator." Thus liberation is not a foreign concept but at the center of the biblical kerygma. By what right, therefore, can present-day liberation theology be accused of being an excrescence of biblical theology? How can "theologians" dare to deny the rights of a "hermeneutics" of the Exodus as a Latin American theological moment? After all, there is *the event* of the Exodus and faith in a God who did something for the *historical* liberation of a people.

b. The mediation of the leader. Why doesn't God save Israel directly, without "calling" Moses? In the history of salvation God avails himself of many human mediations. Indeed, God's presence in *our history* makes manifest the driving forces of this history and orientates them toward God's purposes. On the level of religious narration, Moses is a leader because he was "called" by Yahweh and received the mission to lead Israel out of its bondage. But in fact he was "called" because he was a leader. The interpretation—which explores meaning—inverts the relationship to the form in which it appears in the kerygmatic language.

In the second place, human mediation plays an eminent role in the faith process. Moses must be accepted as God's *emissary;* otherwise liberation cannot come about. According to Exodus 6:9, which we have already considered, the Hebrews "did not listen" to Moses. This meant they were blocking God's plans. It would have made no sense for Yahweh to choose another emissary who enjoyed a greater "credibility" with the Israelites. God reveals himself as much through the event as through a *person*. Moses is a key figure not only because he was the leader who successfully organized and led the departure from Egypt (as mediator) but also because he expresses an essential dimension of faith. It was easier for the Hebrews to believe in Yahweh directly rather than in Moses, a human being like themselves. But this same God expressed himself through Moses, and Moses had to assume *that historical and personal vocation to freedom*. It was not easy.

This theme of faith in the emissary has been so well grasped by the biblical tradition that the whole body of the prophetic literature refers to it (cf. Jeremiah's criticism, 25:3ff.). Faith in the prophet as the emissary of God is the key for understanding the God of history, whose interpreter the prophet is. The Gospel of John is another biblical locus where faith as recognition of the emissary stands out most clearly. Here Jesus is the typological correlate of Moses (see especially John 5:43ff. and the many discussions with the Jews in which Jesus criticizes unbelief *in him* and, consequently, their "not knowing" of the Father). Rabbinical tradition had perfected the biblical datum in this matter, and the discourse of Stephen before the Sanhedrin of Jerusalem exploits this theme: reminding his Jewish listeners that the Hebrews had not believed in Moses even though he had been the leader chosen by God to save Israel, he *now* accuses them of not accepting *Jesus* as the new author of life (Acts 7:20ff., especially vv. 35f. and 51ff.). The Jews of that time, Stephen charges, are doing what their forefathers had done (vv. 51ff.).

Biblical faith, which is not intellectual but dynamic and existential, expresses itself in various dimensions: faith-as-*recognition* of God in the event (theology of the Exodus); faith-as-*commitment* to the given word (in the Covenant); faith-as-*strength* in bearing witness (theology of the Spirit in Luke); faith-as-*openness* to the gift of God (frequent in the synoptic Gospels); faith-as-*acceptance* of the emissary. Each aspect has its richness. In this section we are trying to assess the last mentioned form, linked to the presence of Moses in the liberation account. We can conclude with a reflection relevant to us: catechized in a "terminated" revelation and in a hermeneutical incapacity to recognize *new* forms of God's presence in our own history, we are not prepared to "interpret" the role of certain figures in the history of our peoples. (To profess that God directs history and to trust in God's providence without recognizing his step in the events of liberation is to fashion a theology for the evasion of any commitment.) Christians have so often rejected an "interpreter" of God in the name of an ill-conceived faith. Nevertheless our Latin American history has had, and now has, new Moses-figures who utter their liberating, conscientizing word. Shall we follow them, shall we "interpret" them, or shall we reject them?

c. A consciousness of freedom. The entire Exodus experience made a deep impression on the being of Israel as a very profound experience. Indeed it was the most decisive event in its history; in it Israel grasped a liberating sense of God and an essential value in its own vocation, namely, *freedom*. This explains why the fundamental consciousness of Israel is a consciousness of freedom—at the communal level of the Covenant, or as a people, and at the level of the person. After maturing through prolonged reflection, being collected in the central tradition, and subsequently expressed in the written Word, this experience is elevated to the category of a *message* for all humankind. It is the enunciation of the exemplary event, the announcement of a vocation, the denunciation of all that is not. Such is the value of this kerygma of freedom.

If freedom is one of the intrinsic human values, if the message of the Exodus represents it as a people's essential vocation, then why is there any hesitation to be open to freedom? Why has freedom been nullified in so many traditional forms of Christian life? And here is the most dramatic question of all: Why was the Church so alienated as not to see the signs of the times clearly pointing up the path of liberation? And why does this alienation of times continue today? Why did it collaborate for so long with the agents of the dependency of peoples and treat so many liberation movements as anti-evangelical?

d. Violence. Love and violence are two opposite but connected poles. The irreducible opposition between love and hate is something different. Love can be violent when the loved object cannot be retained or recovered except by force. Love betrayed is also fearsome. Love for the other is "peace" when all is well, but it is "struggle" when injustice is present. "Peace at any price"[10] cannot be justified when the absence of justice makes the "peace-lovers" into spectators of the misery of others. This attitude is proper to the tragic theater, not to Christian praxis.

The history of the Exodus is eminently instructive in this respect. God acts *with vigor:* ". . . I will bring you out from under the burdens of the Egyptians" (Exod. 6:6); "I know that the king of Egypt will not let you go unless compelled by *a mighty hand*" (Exod. 3:19). If the oppression is carried to the extreme of repression, the liberating action is necessarily violent, as is the destruction of the pharaonic hosts, or it is prepared by none too gentle persuasive means, such as the plagues ("Pharaoh will not listen to you; then I will lay my hand upon Egypt . . ." [Exod. 7:4]).

How can we explain that God operates in this violent manner? (And let it not be said that God is the "lord" of human life, because that is to project onto God the "shadow" of the oppressor whom we know and who plays with the lives of others.) God acted violently because the situation of the Hebrews admitted of no other path. At first God tried the peaceful path by having Moses and Aaron petition the king *to allow* their people to go (Exod. 3:18; 5:1; etc.). But the oppressor never liberates. He would cease to be the only thing that he is. The innumerable replies of the pharaoh convincingly attest that any path of liberation is begun from below and goes *against* the oppressing power. The struggle between the two powers is the very essence of the "oppression-liberation" dialectic. Such was the case of all the deeds leading to our independence; they could not be peaceful nor the result of any understanding. Any liberation is achieved when the power of the oppressor is eliminated and another, salvific power is installed. It is the ambivalence of power—salvific by vocation, oppressive by degeneration—that gives meaning to our history of dependence and the processes of liberation.[11]

Let us return to our question: Why does the God of the Exodus act violently? Why did God not respect the lives of the Egyptians, whose king and whose firstborn he sacrificed? Because oppression is *never* justifiable. Injustice can *never* be rationalized. Nor is it "tolerable" through resignation when legal or "peaceful" means to eradicate it are exhausted. Justice is a radical good that demands *of love* (paradoxical as it may seem) a *violent* action. This is a truth so limpid that it shocks us because we have disfigured the image of love. Freedom, for its part, is a gift so intimate and exigent that, when it is obscured or lost, it requires liberation at any price.

The God of peace is *first of all* the God of justice and freedom. Peace is "sinful" when it serves to maintain injustice and dependence. (It is the peak of paradox that those who proclaim peace-in-justice often are the authors and collaborators of the violence of power.) The condemnation of "unjustified violence" is a typical form of "introjecting" the oppressor into the oppressed. Thus religion reappears as the opium of the people. And when the Gospel of authentic love degenerates into an "opium of the Christians," what hope remains for the Christians themselves?

Is not the Exodus theme of immense hermeneutical richness?

CHAPTER III

Created for Freedom (Genesis 1-2)

We should now explain why we include Genesis in our study, and why we do so at this particular point and not at the start. The first book of the Bible—which interprets the "meaning" of human beings in the world from the perspective of their origins, of their fundamental and essential being—makes no mention of liberation. Nevertheless it clearly establishes the reality of the *free* person. Without using the word "freedom" (rarely employed in the biblical lexicon) it institutes freedom as a human *vocation*. But it expresses this vocation in a symbolic language, much more compact and vocative than the common term "free" or "freedom."

In the second place, we turn our attention to Genesis only now because the human vocation spotlighted in its particular language is grasped by virtue of a historical experience of *liberation*. The eloquent pages of Genesis could not have been written without a prior deep reflection on the Exodus event. Genesis is an "interpretation" of Exodus, expressed in the language of the origins, of the ontological "project" of human beings. We know that the Priestly account of Genesis 1 and the Yahwist account of Chapter 2 reflect a theological elaboration developed in the fifth or sixth and tenth centuries B.C., respectively, and that the Pentateuch, in its present form, does not go further back than the fourth or fifth centuries B.C. During these time-spans Israel already had crystallized its consciousness of national being and its spirituality around this climactic and fundamental event—the loftiest and most profound of its existence and its experience of salvation.

Human beings viewed from the perspective of Genesis appear as created for freedom. We can consider their essence and transcendence and their mission in the world. We shall analyze this aspect of Genesis first of all.

1. THE ESSENCE AND TRANSCENDENCE OF HUMAN BEINGS

The most inexhaustible representation of the essence of human beings is that of their creation *in the image of God* (Gen. 1:26). We shall explore its meaning.[1] The assertion that human beings are made in the image of some god was nothing new. This was a fundamental notion in ancient cultures and in the great religious traditions of Egypt and Mesopotamia. But the characteristic element in the oriental texts was to reserve such a privilege to the *king* or pharaoh. Why? Because according to ancient understandings, the king lives in a very special proximity to the divinity. *(a)* The king is a *son of God* (from the moment of his coronation, but not from the moment of his birth!). He is taken up into the bosom of the divinity as his deputy. The gods, indeed, are the "lords" of the earth and of the cosmos, and in the king they have their "image," or shadow, that is a projection of themselves. *(b)* He is the *savior.* His function is to ensure the well-being and the peace of his subjects. Wars are salvific acts through which he re-establishes the collapsed social order of his country. *(c)* By the same token, the king is the absolute *ruler* of his land and his word is definitional and even creational.[2]

What is new about the Genesis account?

Genesis *never* asserts that the king is an "image of God," although it conceives of him with the aforementioned attributes, especially when his figure is projected onto the future in the mythical language that alludes to the Messiah.[3] Such a reservation with respect to the king is significant in fact; Genesis makes an opposite assertion: that *all human beings* are created "in the image of God" (Gen. 1:26: "Let us make man in our image, after our likeness . . ."). In late (or relatively late) Egyptian texts a "democratization" of the idea of the pharaoh as "image" occurs, but, in practice, it does not go beyond the high functionaries. The universalization ushered in by Genesis connotes a different notion, namely, that human beings are not the image of God beginning from a particular moment of their lives (like the coronation of a king), but from their very *creation,* which, in its turn, is "projected" by God in his Word-plan.

To what can we attribute this innovation? There must have been a very clear motivation to invert the "royal ideology" of the whole Orient. Later, when we refer to the break with the mythical worldview we will describe more exactly the ending of the king's privileged status as "image of God." But the question still remains: to what can we attribute the change in worldview? The answer lies in our earlier commentary on the Exodus event: there is a historical experience that determines a new view of God, of the world, and of the human being. Accordingly we assert once more that the conception of the human being in Genesis cannot be understood without the self-understanding that Israel achieved on the basis of the saving Exodus event.

We must add three fundamental clarifications. First, Genesis goes very far beyond those prophets who called Israel the "son" of God (Hos. 11:1: ". . . and out of Egypt I called my son;" cf. Jer. 31:9). The son is the "image" of the father, as the Priestly tradition understands the term "son" when speaking of Adam's first descendants (Gen. 5:1-3). In Genesis 1:26 (also part of the Priestly tradition), on the other hand, *only man* is mentioned, not Israel, and man is mentioned with respect *to God,* not as an image of his forefathers. In the second place, this universalization of the "image of God" appears precisely in a cosmogonic text. The human question thus goes beyond the horizon of Israel. This notion will also provide us with a theme for meditation. And in the third place, we note that the image of God in human beings is not shaken or erased by sin. Human beings are the image of God in their very being and vocation; sin is alien, the work of freedom itself, which sin cannot spoil. That is to say, human beings are *always* free. But this applies to all human beings, not just to some.

What does the theme of the "image" in the context of liberation lead to?

The aforementioned symbol defines the essence of the human being. But it is a representation that must be deciphered. To be the image of something entails incarnating the features of that thing. In our example, the human being must flesh out something of God. But what? We must first define God in order to know what the human being, God's image, is. What is of import here is the description of God *in the very account* of Genesis 1 itself, not that of other passages. The narrative structure is a significant totality in itself.[4] There God is described as *creator*. God's image, human beings, are thus defined through their *creativity,* and this, in turn, includes autonomy and *freedom.*

It is noteworthy that it is the Priestly author of the Pentateuch, the most scrupulous one, who thinks of the human being as the "image" of God. We know the horror that the Hebrews had of any figurative representations of God. For this reason, Genesis 1:26 is even more significant; it must refer to a profound spiritual value—to that vocational *creativity* of the human being—and not to the reproduction of some corporeal attribute of God.

The *creator* God of the Priestly tradition fashions a human being like himself—a *creator*. The human being is the last of God's works, presented as a special creature. What is most significant is that God ceases to create as soon as human beings are placed in the world. It befits *human beings* to express their creativity in the world formed for them.

2. HUMANKIND'S MISSION IN THE WORLD

Human beings, the image of God and prolongations of the Creator, receive their mission to build up the world right away. The Lord charges them to establish *dominion* over the animals and over the earth. These two realms reflect the cultural horizon of that time and involve the two great advances of humankind, namely, the domestication of animals and agriculture. We may be struck by the absence of any reference to technology as such (metallurgy, architecture) which the Yahwist redactor made in Genesis 4:17-22. Nevertheless in Genesis 1:28 subjection of the earth is alluded to in a sentence that is disconnected, incomplete, and indefinite, perhaps because it was interpolated at the time it was formulated. At any rate, because it is indefinite, the expression remains open to interpretation. Either because we are able to "enter" into the text or, especially, because dominion over the world is expressed in the cultural categories of that time, it is up to us to discover in the text a highly telescoped intention of God who makes every person (not the king) lord and master of the entire earth. This dominion is, however, not to be a selfish possession but a *project*. Human beings must manifest their dominion in their *creativity*, by living out their being as "image" of their Creator. But this vocation in the world is meaningless without autonomy and freedom. Let us explore these notions from two complementary, but opposite, angles: the mythical vision and the biblical vision of the world.

3. THE MYTHICAL WORLDVIEW

In myth, the *world* is the key to all; we are speaking of the cosmos as such, that is, *life, force,* and *order* expressed in the rhythms and the phenomena of the universe around us. The sacred is visualized within the cosmos, in all its multiformity. The divine is present everywhere; the sacred breathes through the cosmos. All things are grasped as symbols referring us to what is both transcendent and immanent. Every aspect of the cosmos is a special instance of the sacred (whence the value of polytheism). By the same token, human beings remain polarized through these hierophanies, or manifestations of the divine. Since the sacred shines through the cosmos, human beings are bound to the cosmos in their every action. Somehow, they have no place in it except when sacralizing themselves through rites of passage. Only if we consecrate a harvest can we eat it. We cannot plow the earth without feeling that we are rending the bosom of the Mother-Goddess. Even the political action of the king is subject to ritual. (Ritualization is typical in mythic peoples inasmuch as rites develop in consonance with the rhythms of nature.) Mythic persons are not free, creators in the sense of being aware of a vocation; rather, they are subject to the cosmos. In fact, their actions denote a search for a non-creative security. For that matter the tendency to "cosmicize" themselves also surges up in Christians when they do not define themselves in terms of their autonomous creativity.

4. THE BIBLICAL WORLDVIEW

What do we find in the Hebrew worldview? The key that breaks with the mythic schema is *the idea of creation*. God created the heavens and the earth (Gen. 1:1). God exists before and independently of the cosmos. To what can we attribute this personality of God when in almost all myths God is pre-cosmic, born of chaos or of another God? Israel had the experience of a *personal* God who acts *in history,* who is independent of nature and superior to the gods of other peoples. On the basis of this experience, Israel elaborates the idea of a God different from the world that he creates. This difference is radical, for the world is no longer under the control of the gods but is rather the *locus of human beings* (as we saw in the commentary on Genesis 1:26 and 28). Now human beings do not need to associate themselves with the rhythms of the cosmos in order to imbibe the sacred. God, different from the world, manifests himself in the *events* of history. The Exodus event was indicative in this respect. The relationship between God and human beings is no longer cosmic, but rather dialogical, within a historicity in which human beings are responsible for a destiny but where they are also challenged by the prophets or by the Gospel.

Thus we understand that human beings created in the image of God are free—in their ontological radicality and in their projection onto the world, in their essence and in their vocation. Without freedom—the juridical correlate of which is autonomy—human beings cannot fulfill themselves nor, by the same token, can they carry out God's plan. Here we connect perfectly with Paulo Freire, who sets in bold relief the human vocation "to be more," a vocation that is denied by injustice, by exploitation, by violence, by oppressors, by an unjust order. This is the source of dehumanization, which is contrary to the plan of Genesis 1:26ff. and its consequence, the "to be less" of the oppressed.[5] By the same token, "to free oneself" signifies "to humanize oneself," "to be more" in being and not in money ("to have more" is the dis-ontological illusion of the oppressor). It means that human beings have gone so far as to be "creators," that they are able to exercise dominion over the earth. It means that human beings are able to express the image of God etched as project since the very creation of human beings.

5. FROM THE IDEAL TO THE REALIZATION

A transition occurs between the Exodus event, an *experience* of liberation, and the anthropological worldview of Genesis. (We have dwelt on 1:26ff., but the same human vocation to transform the earth is asserted in 2:5ff. in different language.) From the singular, immensely significant event, the faith of Israel leads to a universal definition for all times. Both poles influence *praxis*, but in different ways. The Exodus event, as salvation from slavery, *impedes* any new form of oppression thenceforth. The consciousness of freedom begins to insert itself into the Hebrew worldview through interpretation of the Exodus and through its memorial in the cult and the institutions. We have already referred to the feast as actualizations of the salvific Exodus event (cf. Exod. 12:14,17, etc.; Deut. 16, especially v. 12 at the conclusion of the prescriptions on the Feast of Weeks: "You shall remember that you were a slave in Egypt"). The Sabbath, a central institution in the life of Israel, according to the Elohist redactor of Exodus 20:11 and the Priestly account of 31:17 has its archetype in God's day of rest after the creation. But for the Deuteronomist author the archetype lies in the liberation from Egyptian bondage: "You shall remember that you were a servant in the land of Egypt, and the Lord your God brought you out thence with a mighty hand and an outstretched arm; therefore the Lord your God commanded you to keep the sabbath day" (Deut. 5:15). The cult and the sacred customs have a very profound consciousness-raising function. Israel had the privilege of forming its conscience in the line of freedom. Later, we shall see how this preparation was to contribute to the interpretation of the Christian Easter and how Easter *must be* profoundly consciousness-raising in our context as oppressed peoples.

Nevertheless cult can be a substitute for praxis. How was this liberating mentality of the Exodus manifested in Israelite customs? The Pentateuch tells us that the Hebrews did not practice slavery *among themselves*—surely as a reflection of the theology of the Exodus, lived at the level of the *people*. Even when a Hebrew sold himself as a slave to another, the latter had to free him in the seventh year (legislative texts in Lev. 25:39ff. and Deut. 15:21ff.). Curiously, the acquisition or retention of slaves "from among the nations that are round about you" (Lev. 25:44; cf. Jos. 9:23, 27) was quite permissible. In this case the "vocation to freedom," to "be more," claimed *for all people* in the ideological passage of Genesis, was not implemented in Israelite social praxis. It always happens that praxis draws inspiration from an ideal or a worldview, but it never attains their total actualization. We find a similar gap between the Gospel as message and the praxis of Christians. But, it is for this very reason that the ideal of the Gospel or the orienting message of Genesis are important. They are the Word that summons, which at any moment can seize the prophet to denounce the crooked path or to announce benediction.

These reflections call for a final observation: together with the vocational word of Genesis 1 or the summoning word of the Gospel, there is the "memorial" of the concrete event of an archetypical liberation, namely, the Exodus (the prohibition of slavery is justified with these words in Deut. 15:15: "You shall remember that you were a slave in the land of Egypt, and the Lord your God redeemed you; *therefore* I command you this today") and the Paschal mystery, which demands the liberation of self and others in all dimensions (we shall treat this when we consider Paul's letter to the Romans).

In conclusion: human beings are called to freedom for themselves and for others; it is an ontological vocation, and humankind has been liberated programmatically by God in an event of salvation history.

6. SOME REFLECTIONS

Although we do not wish to interrupt the reader's hermeneutical inspiration—indeed our intention is to promote it—we shall express some reflections here that we have already tested in group discussions.

a. In the anthropological worldview of the Bible, human beings are created in the image of the Creator as free and autonomous beings on the earth. What perspectives are deducible from this for the self-understanding of Christians in today's world? Does the Church offer people the possibility to be free? Or is the Word of God "paganized" within the Church and in the structures of the present-day world? (Recall what we said above about the mythical worldview.)

We are asking, in effect, whether we have gauged the meaning and the exigencies of being free, and the implications of the vocation to freedom and autonomy in the world. The structures of the present-day world provide privileges to the few and oppress the many. We can speak of a "structural sin," to the liberation from which "western and Christian" civilization has contributed very little, if it is not, indeed, its very antonomastic expression.

Also the subjection of the earth (of nature) by technology and science can open the path to human well-being and to spiritual realization through the use of intelligence, but it can also usher in oppression. There is a progressism yearning for the infinite that stifles human beings as an infinity of "desire" itself, the "infinite evil" of which Ricoeur speaks.[6] So we understand that human creativity is ambiguous: it can continue the creation of God and make for a better world, or it can destroy others.

The Third World in particular suffers the consequences of the warping of the ideal of Genesis 1:26ff. Creative technology, marvelous as it is, develops *from* and *for* certain rich, capitalist countries, producing a constantly increasing impoverishment of the poorer countries. To top it all, our consumer society also fascinates the poor and seems to be made to sell what is produced by the rich countries or companies, which extract the natural wealth of the poor countries. In Latin America the fraud of "foreign investments," as an aid or support for development, is added to these evils. What is certain is that for each dollar that comes into these Latin American countries, two or more are taken out, according to recent and alarming statistics.[7]

b. We also wonder whether that transcendent image of the human being has not become a cause of alienation in the life of the Church instead of being the motive force of a liberation. The question applies to any religious context. In fact, there is a tendency in religious persons, precisely because they value the transcendent (a valoration that in itself is significant), to fall into the same contradiction that we have noted in regard to creativity. In this case, it leads to the loss of the historical sense, giving a disproportionate importance to the divine as the only dimension. To be the image of God is then interpreted as a vocation to the eternal and a negation of the historical (the typical gnostic contamination of Christianity). This same extrapolation to the transcendent "froze" human liberty in a tangle of laws and traditions that stifled creativity. To top it all, certain forms of alienation of freedom were (and in part are) maintained—through a retrospective forming of consciousness—as manifestations of a "state of perfection." In our treatment of the New Testament we shall return to the fundamental theme of religious alienation as the source of many others. But we wish to signal its profound relationship to a total vision of the human being that loses sight of the kerygma of Genesis. This kerygma once again challenges us Christians.

c. Finally, is there not a "paganization" (we have already mentioned the theme) in the structures of the present-day world, the heir of Christianity, and even within the very life of the Church? There is another tendency in the human beings, that of "cosmicizing" themselves, of reverting to a mythical mentality. A specific example is the social or liturgical ritualism that binds people to such an extent and makes them lose sight of the meaning of the event. Ritual is another ambiguous value: good in itself (when the "word" that gives it intentionality prevails), it becomes negative when it abandons the prophetic element of the message and the opus operatum prevails, independently of a praxis committed to reality. That our Christianity is rapidly "depaganizing" itself is a grace of God. We believe that this process is deeper in Latin America, because of new critical consciousness that has its starting point in lived situations and not in academic issues. In this itinerary of liberation, we wish to call attention to the contribution signified by a re-reading of the motif of the human being as "image of God." Its implications focus the whole theology of the liberation experience of the Exodus; at the same time, they introduce a call to the historical commitment to transform the world in freedom and to re-understand oneself in this freedom *for creativity*. As such, the Genesis theme signals an opening in the spectrum of liberation, an idea to which we shall return in the last part of this essay.

CHAPTER IV

The Prophet, "Conscientizer" of Alienated Humanity

A reference to the prophets cannot be omitted in a hermeneutics of liberation. Three reasons compel their inclusion: their attitude in the face of the "situation" of the people, their denunciation of oppressors, their capacity to distinguish the good from the bad in religious traditions. Summing up each function in a single suggestive word, we shall say that the prophets are the interpreters of the times (inscribing themselves therefore in the line of the hermeneutics of the Exodus), the critics of the sin and falsehood of Israel, and the conscientizers of inauthentic and alienated human beings. These three expressions of prophetism have much to do with any process of liberation.

This may explain why we Latin Americans feel that the biblical prophets are so close to us and why we are so aware of the resurgence of the prophetic role in the new Church; this is a Church that is born, expresses itself, and matures only by inserting itself in the whole life of human beings, from the social realm to the political to the spiritual. The prophets are the qualified exponents of a political faith. It is difficult to find any oracle—if there be one—that defines eternal values that are not manifested socially. The principal cause is twofold: the prophets always refer to Israel or to its representatives *as a people,* whose existence always touches upon the political and the wielders of power; in the second place, they are speaking to a people *committed* to their God beginning with the liberating and "acquisitive" exodus event (note the many words on "ransom," "redemption," etc., and Eph. 1:14).

The three dimensions that we wish to spotlight in the prophet add something specific to the themes of Exodus and vocation, which we have already analyzed. We maintained that the event of the liberation from Egypt was "interpreted." The prophet is also a hermeneutist of that liberation. What difference is there? In other words, why were there no prophets in the first centuries after the Exodus? Why do they arise when Israel abandons its communitarian confederation of tribes and adopts the form of a centralized, monarchical government? Who was the interpreter of events in the light of the Exodus in those first centuries?

I believe that the explanation is simple—unless I err by ingenuousness: in a fecund moment, close to the salvific experience of the Exodus, *the community itself* began "saying its word." Living in the plenitude of the event, the community began to interpret it in light of its new experiences of liberation (in Transjordan, in the conquest of the land, in the epoch of the struggles against the neighboring kingdoms with the Judges). The introduction to the great Jeremiahan oracle (2:2-3) magnificently illustrates the youthful fidelity of Israel: "Thus says the Lord, I remember the devotion of your youth, your love as a bride, how you followed me in the wilderness, in a land not sown, Israel was holy to the Lord, the first fruits of his harvest. All who ate of it became guilty; evil came upon them." Its parallel is that of the first Christian *community,* suffused with the Paschal experience, full of dynamism and totally faithful to the Word. The church in one case and the people of Israel in the other were a *community* that lived *as such* and that, for this very reason, "interpreted" the originary salvific event (Easter and the Exodus respectively).

But when the community—the people in its political expression—split and the wielders of power began to play an essential role (the king in Israel, Constantianism and later the outsized hierarchy in the Church) the central event was no longer interpreted in all its purity and dynamism and as the constant summons to the recognition of God. Rather, the decisions and the "words" of the wielders of power protect their own interests. The phenomenon is characteristic. Moreover, the wielders of power separate themselves from the people, the hierarchy from the community. The community, the people, either preserve their profound capacity "to make history," to be faithful to the call of God, or they are disorientated by those who govern them.

This gives rise to the necessity for the prophet, whose voice interprets history in a different way. The prophets place themselves *in confrontation with* the power structure, and almost always from within the community or the people. The prophets are never from among power elite; they rise from the grassroots or, at least, speak on the basis of their identification with these bottommost strata. Even when they criticize *the people* of Israel, they do not do so as power-holders but by using the single weapon of their word: "Behold, I have put my words in your mouth. See, I have set you this day over *nations* and over *kingdoms,* to pluck up and to break down, to destroy and to overthrow, to build and to plant" (Jer. 1:9f.).

Let us briefly view how the prophets act in their triple dimension (more schematic than complete).[1] They denounce the loss-of-meaning of the past liberation of the Exodus; they denounce the present oppression of the weak; and they foretell the future oppression of the exile as punishment for a massive infidelity to history, which they have aborted as a project of salvation.

Our survey will be brief because what follows is not new and others have dealt very thoroughly with it. The example of the prophets is of great topicality for a commitment to liberation, and liberation theology has seen in it an inexhaustible source of inspiration in its message.

1. THE PROPHET, "CRITIC" OF ISRAEL

The first prophetic accusation against the people of Israel is that they have abandoned Yahweh and returned to "strange gods," typified in Baal. The one sin has two sides to it, and Jeremiah stigmatizes it as a twofold iniquity: "For my people have committed two evils; they have forsaken me, the fountain of living waters, and hewed out cisterns for themselves, broken cisterns, that can hold no water" (2:13). The prophets do not defend fidelity to Yahweh because they are monotheists; they are not dogmatic. In fact, it is the other way around: monotheism is expressed insofar as Israel recognizes in the God of the Exodus its *only* savior. Yahweh is the God of salvific events, and Israel does not have a similar experience with other gods (note Elijah's eloquent prayer atop Mount Carmel, in which he invokes Yahweh as God "of the Fathers" and of Israel, of the Promise and of liberation; 1 Kings 18:36). Thus the prophet denounces the grievous *sin* of Israel, "harlotry" as the judicious Hosea sees fit to call it (Hos. 1:2; 2:1ff.; cf. Ezek. 16:14ff.; 23:1ff.). On the one hand, this sin of infidelity is an act of ingratitude (Jer. 2:5ff.; Amos 2:9ff.; Mic. 6:3-5; etc.) and, on the other, a "paganization" in the direction of the cosmic gods. Above all, it obscures God's historical plan. The prophet criticizes this infidelity to the historical vocation of humankind.

What are the specific sins that undo God's plan as disclosed in the Exodus? The turn to Baal is not only a general attitude. As a loss of a particular vocation and as an alienation to cosmic forces, it is a concrete sin. Yahweh then has no meaning for Israel. Together with this, or separately, the prophets constantly and vigorously indict social *injustices*. The denunciation of the oppression of the weak (the poor, and the defenseless before the law, who are usually the same) is implacably clear in the voices of Amos, Isaiah, and Jeremiah, but it is not difficult to find it in the other spokesmen of Yahweh.

Amos. In the celebrated oracles against the nations neighboring Israel, Amos accuses them of war crimes (1:1-2:3). But he criticizes Israel for its sins of injustice and of oppression against the poor: "they that trample the head of the poor into the dust of the earth, and turn aside the way of the afflicted" (2:7). The wives of the potentates of Samaria, who are compared to the fat cows of Bashan (a fertile region of the Transjordan), are upbraided because they "oppress the poor" and "crush the needy" and because of their lust for luxury and dissipation (4:1-5). In the central oracle of chapter 5 he exposes bribe-taking judges, their expropriations of houses and fields, their consequent illicit enrichment, their transgressions against the poor (5:10-13); "O you who turn justice to wormwood and cast down righteousness to the earth!" (5:7). We see that the denunciation is directed against those who wield "power."

Isaiah. The monarchy introduces privileges and these beget new injustices, one of which is the latifundia, or large landed estates: "Woe to those who join house to house, who add field to field, until there is no more room, and you are made to dwell alone in the midst of the land" (Isa. 5:8). Other forms of oppression are denounced in the introductory oracle, which summarizes the preaching of the Jerusalemite prophet (cf. verses 21-23). The high and the mighty are also recriminated (3:12-26) in a terrible prediction of punishment for having misled *the people,* thus perverting their function: ("My *people—* children are their oppressors, and women rule over them . . . ; *O my people,* your leaders mislead you . . ." (3:12); to the leaders: ". . . you have devoured the vineyard [an image of the people, cf. 5:1ff.], the spoil of the poor is in your houses. What do you mean by crushing *my people,* by grinding the face of the poor?" 3:14ff.). The people are ruined by those who lead them. The *perversion of power* is a constant motif in the prophetic denunciation.

Jeremiah. He is the accuser by antonomasia of the king of Jerusalem. His testimony is notable inasmuch as he was active at the beginning of the exile of 597. He criticizes the sin of all Judah especially in his first utterances (as in the "memorandum" of the apostasy in chapter 2; cf. chap. 3ff.). But we should remember that he pronounces his oracles in the capital, Jerusalem, the site from which the means of power are managed and in which the prevailing ideology has its source. The people tend to "paganize" themselves on their own, but they do so even more rapidly under the influence of the example set by the great urban centers. In 7:1ff., Jeremiah also threatens the inhabitants of Jerusalem, in a discourse against the temple on which we shall comment later.

At any rate, Jeremiah specializes, as it were, in denouncing the kings of Jerusalem for their crooked conduct. We shall refer only to the scenes of chapters 22 and 36. He sets before Jehoiakim the example of his father, Josiah, who treated the poor and the needy with justice; Jehoiakim, on the other hand, oppresses and practices violence on his subjects (22:16f.). On another occasion, this fatidic king, in the presence of his officials, burns the prophet's written message (36:23, 27); but Jeremiah, in very plain letters written on a new scroll, reiterates the divine plan to liquidate his dynasty: "He shall have none to sit upon the throne of David and his dead body shall be cast out to the heat by day and the frost by night. . ." (36:30). He reminds the same king, or his successor of a few days (Jehoiachin), of his function to "do justice and righteousness, and deliver from the hand of the oppressor . . . and do no wrong or violence" (22:3f.); he repeats this demand before Zedekiah, a puppet of the Babylonians and the last king of Jerusalem (22:12).

The issue always revolves around those who hold power and who pervert it. In 22:16 Jeremiah uses a very significant expression: after citing Josiah's acts of justice toward the oppressed, he exclaims: "Is not this to *know me,* says the Lord." The relation is of a very profound significance and takes for granted the whole theology of the Exodus. Israel has "known" God in his work of liberation. Thenceforth "to know" God entails living the liberation and liberating others. For the king it entails practicing "justice" toward the poor and lowly. Indeed, the king represents Yahweh. To practice oppression is tantamount to "not knowing" the God who has given freedom. The Christian "re-reading" of this prophetic expression is very clear. This is the thrust of the repeated phrase "when did we know thee?" in Matthew 25:37ff. It is only to those who work for the liberation of the oppressed that Christ can say: "Is this not to *know me?*" But who, in our Latin America, can we surmise is hearkening to that prophetic voice.[2]

2. THE PROPHET, "CONSCIENTIZER" OF THE PEOPLE

This dimension of the prophet is connected with the other two (critique and interpretation of history), but it also has an importance of its own and must be set in bold relief because of its topicality. We know that there is no process of liberation without a stage of conscientization in the oppressed people; they alone can take the step toward freedom and toward "being more." To conscientize means to unmask what is false, on the one hand, and to be situated in reality, on the other. One can "criticize" the sin of the oppressors (prophetic denunciation) and "conscientize" the oppressed so that they may liberate themselves. This perhaps is the schema that we would like always to apply. But the criticism of the oppressors conscientizes the oppressed who hear it; the conscientization of the oppressed comes into being as a crisis of the oppressors. By their *criticisms* the prophets conscientize not only the people, but also, and especially, their leaders.

The prophets situate themselves on the religious plane, of course, in order to focus on the social sphere. They speak to a people knowledgeable about their vocation and the Covenant. The prophets do not presuppose a "closed consciousness"[3] that must be opened by arousing a *critical* consciousness of reality in their hearers. A hermeneutical transposition is legitimate here. Nevertheless we wish to state that Israel's sinful consciousness was equivalent to a consciousness "closed" to the knowledge of God in history and to the realization of his justice (Jer. 7:5ff.), as we have pointed out. It was a falsified consciousness, the source of inauthentic attitudes. By unmasking the deceitful intentions, the prophets stimulate thinking about the bared underlying reality. They raise consciousness. Rarely do they speak indirectly to the people about the oppressor (for example, Jer. 5:26ff.). Their language is directly accusatory, and as they denounce they also clarify. Several episodes will illustrate this.

"Peace." At all times there are true and false prophets. How are they distinguished? Deuteronomy codified the "marks" of credibility (18:21f.), but they were unsatisfactory: false prophets also worked prodigies and were able to pass themselves off as emissaries of Yahweh. The important thing was that the prophets should, in fact, speak in the name of the God of the Covenant,

whose demands and maledictions were known. This was why Israel, as the transgressor of justice, could hope for nothing but exile. The prophets were genuine if they inverted the terms, thereby justifying wicked conduct.

Jeremiah's dispute with his "shadow" Hananiah (28:1ff., especially v. 9), and later with other false prophets (23:9ff.) is indicative. The false prophets say "peace," "no evil shall come upon you" to those who do not hearken to the word of God (v. 17!). Thus, the prophets "conscientize" in that they disclose where truth is concealed and aid their hearers to situate themselves in reality and to take this reality unto themselves (the entire chapter 28 of Jeremiah is suggestive in this respect). The prophets who denounce, not those who flatter, are the emissaries of God. Those who are for the Covenant, and not for the oppressors, are the true prophets. Those who interpret the Gospel and "denounce" the sin of the powerful or even of the Church itself stand in this great prophetic tradition, not those who defend the unjust social order, however "western and Christian" it may be. Some theologies of secularization of the rich countries can be "narcotizers" and say "peace" to the oppressors.[4]

The inversion of values. The second chapter of Jeremiah, which provides the context of Jeremiah 2:13 on the twofold sin of Judah, demonstrates how people are deceived by the appearances of reality itself. Baal was an important deity, lord of the phenomena of life; his cult must have both impressed and tempted the Jews. But the prophet shows them that things are not as they seem, that *Yahweh*, the author of Israel's vocation and of so many salvific interventions since the Exodus, could also be discovered in natural phenomena ("They did not say, 'Where is the Lord who brought us from the land of Egypt? . . . ,' " v. 6; "*I* introduced you into a *plentiful land . . . ,*" v. 7). The prophet reinverts the subversion of values of a misguided popular religiosity. He subsumes it into an historical experience of liberation (as a human project), rescuing it from a syncretism that distorts the kerygma. In this, as in many other accusatory oracles, the prophet stimulates thinking; he re-forms consciousness. Let us note that the example given is of a great relevance for the Latin American problems of popular religiosity. In what sense and with what new richness might it be assimilated—not rejected—into a liberation project of autochthonous people?

There are other biblical elements for the discussion of the problem, but for the present there is no need to add more.[5]

The cult. All the great prophets said their word against the official cult of Jerusalem (Isa. 1:11-17; Jer. 7:2ff.; 26:2ff.; Amos 5:21-27; Hos. 6:6; Mic. 6:6-7). The cult, like many sacred values, is ambiguous; in itself it is good. (The Priestly tradition of Exodus 25ff. goes back to Sinai itself.) Cult is linked to the memorial of the liberator God, as we have already seen. But it can be perverted: if it becomes lifeless it turns into mere formalism, concealing an inner vacuum. This happens only too frequently. But the prophets denounce not so much the "emptiness" of the ritualist cult as the concealment, through it, of a sin essentially antithetical to the cult *of Yahweh*, the God of the Exodus. This sin is the sin of *oppression*.

On reading the cited passages we discover the harshness of the accusation ("I have had enough of burnt offerings . . ."; "who requires of you? . . ."; "seek justice, correct oppression; defend the fatherless, plead for the widow"; Isa. 1:11ff.). By multiplying their offerings—ill-gotten by the spoliation of the poor—the oppressors pose as "righteous"; by helping the temple they appear as "benefactors." This has been so common among the rich and the proprietors of great wealth and landed estates in our own situation that any comment is superfluous. Our interest is to highlight this conscientizing force of the prophets. Their word unmasks the inauthenticity of the oppressors (and not only the ingenuous ones) who falsify the august and profound meaning of cult as a celebration of the God of the oppressed.

The great changes of our times are also due to a progressive conscientization that did not come from within the structures—we repeat that the oppressor never liberates—but from an authentic living of the Gospel. It is noteworthy that Catholics who are traditional and most averse to change are those who are also most faithful to ritualism, while Christians committed to liberation live sporadic and spontaneous—but more profound—forms of the cult. This also gives us pause for thought.

There are other instances of the "conscientizing" prophet: the denunciation of the pact with Egypt (Jeremiah) or with Assyria (Hosea) as useless and traitorous to the people because, like inauthentic cult, it conceals a grave infidelity toward the God of *the* Covenant. Bible readers can recall and ponder their own examples.

3. THE PROPHET, INTERPRETER OF HISTORY

The prophets do not speak at a distance, of a remote future; they dialogue with a people or with the kings of their own time. The eschatological hope—touched on in so many prophetic oracles—opens up *from within* history and as a *present* response to it. Now if God manifests himself in historical events (the Exodus clearly tells us that) and these are irreversible, the *continuum* of the salvific plan is understood and expressed through "interpretation." This gives rise to the prophet's function. Moreover, this manner of self-manifestation of the biblical God entails a perennially new epiphany. Basic to all of this is an attitude of faith that permits us to "recognize" the step of God through engagement in life and historical commitment. The savior God is discovered in the process of the liberation of the oppressed if we find ourselves in a world of oppression. *It is there* that we understand the Lord. This is our condition and perhaps our privilege of being able to hear and follow God.

We had accustomed ourselves to easier ways of "knowing" God: dogmatic definitions, a Gospel read outside of history, a literal interpretation of the Bible, etc. None of this is negative; everything has value and is essential—but insofar as it is *subsumed* into an experience of God in the "signs of the times." It was simpler to interpret the will of God (concerning history!) through "apparitions" to certain saints or privileged persons. We Christians have rested content in the revelations of the Virgin of Fatima, hoping for the "conversion of Russia" with a remnant of an apocalyptic mentality. We needed only to do penance, and God would regulate matters. The fundamental posture should have been to ask ourselves why Russia is communist, to cooperate with the advent of an authentic, profound socialism, to see in Marxism a "sign of the times" that awakens the "subversive memory" of the Exodus in the Christians instead of being frightened by Russian "atheism."

When Christians are slow in interpreting the great events of the world, God continues to act with other names. Is the flowering of other "Marxisms" in the world not a denunciation of the inoperativeness of Christians, exhausted in the liberal capitalist worldview of the "Christian" West? Are not the movements of national liberation in Latin America a response to the spread of communist ideologies (which in their negative manifestation can cover new forms of dependence)? It is here that Christians are getting involved with all the dynamism of their faith. The faith gives them the prophetic gift of recognizing the opportune time (the *kairos*) of salvation. The prophets, the interpreters of history, unquestionably were not an exclusive privilege of Israel. Wherever God speaks through events, there the prophet's presence is the key. The advantage for us Christians is that Pentecost has poured out the prophetic Spirit *in the community* (Acts 2:16ff.). Fundamentally it can work only in the people-of-God on the march; in Latin America today this means in the people committed in faith to the projects of liberation.

The triple dimension of the biblical prophet—critic, conscientizer, and interpreter—has much to do with a hermeneutics of liberation.

4. PROPHECY AND POLITICS

A final question arises: why were the prophets of Israel not political leaders or revolutionaries? Why did they not organize any liberation movement against so many oppressor-kings? What good was their Word?

We shall reply in two ways: the first, from a direct reading of the prophets; the second, from a hermeneutical perspective. First, the prophets, *per se*, are not commanders or leaders. Their strength is in the denouncing, conscientizing, orientating *word*—a committed word to be sure. We do not know what might have resulted from this word. Moreover, the prophets move on the religious plane: they recall the commitment of the Covenant—a concrete social commitment—but they wait for the action *of God* when the oppressor or the sinner does not change. The prophets expect *conversion*, an attitude that is both most profound and, at bottom, most revolutionary. In this ideological framework no thought is given to the way of revolutionary politics. Nor are there any ideological means or any structural conditioning for such a way. We shall see that the same question is posed in regard to the New Testament.

Second, the hermeneutical response is involved with the same issues. Other social and political conditions; another mentality; other instruments of the strategy of power; the consciousness of the fundamental strength of the *people;* even the democratic forms of political action: all these permit a new reflection on prophetic action in the oppressed or dependent world. The prophetic voice resounds with the same power, but with new expressions. Given its nature—the call of the Covenant that commits to love—it can and must release other effects. Present-day prophets, involved in a liberating mission, must have the light to discern the signs of the times.

CHAPTER V

The Christ, "Liberator" of the Oppressed

With regard to the New Testament we shall limit ourselves to two points, one practical (the Gospels) and the other doctrinal (St. Paul), trying to see their complementarity. Paul centers his theology on the paschal mystery, both because of its centrality and because his experience of Christ was paschal: he had not known Jesus personally. The Apostles or the evangelists, on the other hand, describe Jesus of Nazareth. And although the redaction of the Gospels is hermeneutical—and as such was done in the light of the paschal event—we can clearly recognize the contours of this august figure who was Christ, the liberator, from the moment of his prophetic consecration at his baptism in the Jordan to the drama of his own death for the cause of human liberation.

We can discern Jesus' actions and words in the story of his life. We will consider certain episodes that are illustrative for the theme that concerns us. In no way is it our intention to be complete and exhaustive. Christians should know the Gospel; here it is solely a matter of spotlighting certain aspects of the gospel message, some well known, others being re-presented, as it were, because they are now viewed from an oppression-liberation perspective. Concretely, our reflections will focus on the following points: Jesus' orientation toward his death-commitment, his actions, then his liberative words, the message of the Beatitudes, his trial, and finally some general concluding observations.

1. FROM THE MESSIAH TO THE SUFFERING SERVANT

In Jesus the Gospels show us a very special path, lineally oriented—from its first manifestations through word and sign—to his death-resurrection. Even more archetypically, he is anointed at baptism in the Spirit of the Word; but his baptism gives him the vocation of the Servant of the celebrated Isaian canticles: proclaimer of a Covenant, light of nations, convoker of the people oppressed in foreign lands, delivered up to death (Isa. 42:1-4; 49:1-13;

50:4-9; 52:13-53:12). The voice over the Jordan that proclaims, "This is my beloved Son, with whom I am well pleased," is the voice that elects the "servant" of the Lord (Isa. 42:1). This vocation is programmatic, and it will displace the immediatist and political meaning of his messianic function. The "Messiah" was the genuine liberator of the people according to Jewish expectations. And Peter recognizes him in the person of Jesus (Mark 8:29); later the high priest wants to know from the lips of Christ himself if he is the Messiah (14:61). He does not deny it, but on both occasions he diverts attention: to the theme of suffering in the scene with Peter (8:31ff.), and to the glory of the Son of Man during the trial in Jerusalem (14:62). Moreover, he imposes silence on Peter and on the others: "And he charged them to tell no one about him" (8:30). This was not to keep the Romans from finding out about him but because he wanted to prepare his disciples for a deeper discovery about him.

The same figure of the triumphant Son of Man (cf. Mark 14:62 and Dan. 7:13ff.) would be manifested at the end *through the sign of the cross*. In other words Jesus, from the moment of his baptism, bears the mark of the "suffering Servant"—who is also the liberator of the oppressed in the "intentioning" oracles of Deutero-Isaiah. And Jesus expresses this vocation in his actions and utterances (see Matthew's remark in the middle of his Gospel [12:14-27], when he cites a text precisely on the Servant). And Jesus does so with a total commitment that culminates in his trial for "subversion."

2. THE "LIBERATING" ATTITUDES OF JESUS

Christ does not speak to accomplish some mission: He speaks from his very self, from his manner of working. Hence the weight of his Word. As we shall show in the following section, his word is conscientizing within the very core of an event, of an action, of a protest on the part of the Pharisees. His word is always contextual; it is not the literary context of the evangelists but that of his own life-witness. Indeed we can almost say that the actions and words of Jesus should be discussed simultaneously. But here we shall consider the context within which his activity unfolded, in order subsequently to understand better his word-in-the-event.

Jesus, in a courageous and typical manner, works on the sabbath. This institution offers him a privileged situational framework for the discernment of values. He opposes "liberating action" to the "rest" of a false consciousness. It is in the Gospel of John that the vocabulary of "work" is used most frequently. Jesus identifies himself with the Father, who is always "working" (5:17). He affirms this on the occasion that the Jews criticize him for curing the paralytic at the pool on the sabbath (15:1-16). He puts himself in a "danger zone," but he does so intentionally, since he wants to expose the loss of the primal meaning of the sabbath institution. Let us note that those who are scandalized by Jesus—even though he is doing good—are the ones who define themselves as the guardians of sacred structures. In the example of

John 5, the reply of Jesus is *theological:* he is equal to the Father and the latter is above the sabbath ("My Father is working still, and I am working," v. 17). This further inflames the Jews, who now are scandalized by his profession of equality with God (v. 18). In the Gospel of Matthew, or in the other Synoptics, the replies of Jesus are expressed on an *anthropological* level, without thereby ceasing to be theological, as we shall see. The sabbatical context is the same.

Jesus works on the sabbath, a gesture that provokes the Pharisees. It lays bear their alienation, the oppression of consciences, their characteristic scandal at liberating actions. The present-day equivalents of the sabbath should not be sought precisely in the Sunday rest; such an investigation would be based on merely external concordances. Indeed, the transgression of the obligation of Sunday rest offends less than other transgressions of what is most scrupulously safeguarded as, for example, "authority" coming from God; such authority has a superstructural representation with a biblical base, but it has been ideologically distorted. The correlates of the authority are the obedience of those who have no voice and the "law and order" established and consecrated through the work and magic of an alien tradition. We could extend the list of the "equivalents" of the attitudes of Jesus, focused at this particular moment on the sabbath.

Are there other instances of liberating actions? Jesus conspicuously visits the sick, the lowly, the sinners, children, foreigners. All these persons suffer from a lack of something: health, life-prospects, prestige in the eyes of the "just," abilities, acceptance among the Jews. They are all marginalized. And if they have any value, they cannot express it: the poor because nobody assists them or does them justice; the others because "religious society" punctiliously excludes them.

We can get even closer to the root of this situation, explaining the fury of the Pharisees against Jesus and his deliberate confrontation with them. They are the "just," those who know the will of God and faithfully observe it. Accordingly they can judge others. These three aspects—knowledge, justice, judgment—are correlated, and in the order given here. Each is the foundation for the next. But therein lies their deepest flaw. Their praxis is based on the Law, not on love. Their certainty does not derive from commitment to the event of God, but from their "gnosis," from their knowledge of the Law. They had the key to the truth. Paul was to express this very clearly, as we shall see in the following chapter.

Here we note that the categories of persons enumerated above are excluded from the kingdom by the Pharisees because of their want of "knowledge" of the law. These were sinners who did not know or practice the Law; sickness was considered a consequence of sin (see John 9:2, where the disciples ask about the "sin" of the man born blind or the reply of Jesus to the sick man he cured by the pool in John 5:14, or the paralytic in Matthew 9:2). The Jews marginalized the sick; the Old Testament contains no legislation in their behalf, whereas Leviticus afflicts them even more by requiring them to make atonement for their "sin" (see the case of the leper in Lev. 14:19). Christ conspicuously rejects the sick-sin relation in John 9:2; but even if he accepts it, he directly approaches the sick and cures them. This is a sign of the messianic times as is observed in the Gospels, in the Acts, and in the Pauline gift of healing.

Children were not favored by society; they had no "word" and no account was taken of them. But the Pharisees excluded them for a different reason, namely, for their *ignorance* of the Law. Jesus, on the other hand, does take them into account; he blesses them and affirms their simplicity that makes them "clean" before God (cf. Matt. 18:1-11). Foreigners were despised (and the Samaritans "hated") because they did not possess knowledge of the God of Israel and because of the "political" consequences deriving from this situation. And the poor? Wise and ancient prescriptions provided them with a relative protection (cf. Deut. 15:7ff. and other passages in which there is mention of "the poor, the orphan, and the widow," with frequent mention of the "stranger" as well). But these prescriptions must not have been a primary concern in the time of Christ, since he presents himself as the Savior of the poor, and this is the sign that he is the emissary of God.

The scene described in Matthew 11:1-6 is very suggestive ("and the poor have good news preached to them. And blessed is he who takes no offense at me," vv. 5ff.). The emissary (Messiah) was not expected to be speaking along these lines. He was awaited as the liberator of *Israel* from its political dependency. Christ begins with the liberation *of the poor*. The expression "people of the land" that was originally applied to the poorest folk who had remained on Palestinian soil when the Babylonians deported the skilled stratum of the population (technicians, workers, etc.; cf. 2 Kings 24:14) came to mean those displaced from the religious society of Jerusalem.[1] Uninstructed in the Law, they seemed to be excluded from salvation.

Now Jesus addresses himself to all the marginalized people, doubly oppressed by human egoism in general and by the "religious" structure in particular. He begins his liberation by giving value to their persons. They, too, are *human beings,* but oppressed. We will see in the following section that Jesus' word interprets his liberating actions, denouncing the oppressors and conscientizing the oppressed. The oppressed thus begin their rise from the obscurity of their "being less" to their "being more," of their being the "New Person."

Even more, the gesture of Jesus was to be in solidarity with the poor, to be *one of them*. Only on the basis of this identification could he carry out the work of liberation.[2] Jesus had the experience of being marginalized, denounced, accused, and plotted against by the centers of power. He had no structural or institutional defense. He always moved about at the grassroots level. There is a great difference between becoming rich or powerful to liberate the rich and the powerful, and becoming poor and oppressed to liberate the poor and the oppressed. The former is a contradiction and merely consolidates the mechanisms of domination. The latter is liberating because the poor and the dominated are the raison d'etre of the oppressors.

3. THE "CONSCIENTIZING" WORD OF JESUS

On the basis of his solidarity with the poor and through his appreciation of persons and their values, Jesus conscientizes through his unique Word. He clears the path obstructed by traditions, the Law, and other structures so that *the human being* can emerge. On *this* level—in the encounter of one human being with another—the oppressed and the oppressors alike are liberated. The oppressed affirm their deepest authenticity so that the "shadow" of the oppressors disappears. The oppressors, finding themselves without their opposite pole, remain in their own alienation—from which they can be freed if they accept the profound conversion offered them by God through his emissary.

Matthew 12 provides us with a good set of guidelines on which to reflect. A sequence of actions and utterances of Jesus gradually build up to a core-of-meaning that develops into a "crisis" through which human beings are discerned on a new plane. Those who had the "light," those who passed judgment, suddenly find themselves naked before the Truth, judged by the Light (12:31ff. and 38ff.). Let us see how Jesus acts in concrete situations in which oppressors and oppressed confront each other in action.

The first episode is that of the picking of grain on the sabbath (12:1-8). The Pharisees care not a whit that the disciples of Jesus are hungry; their only concern is that they observe the law. And they point it out to the disciples' master, who, according to them, should take this transgression into account. Jesus replies with three references to Scriptures. Since the Pharisees have recalled a sacred law, he demonstrates the exclusiveness and onesidedness of their interpretation. David transgressed the law that reserved to priests the eating of showbread (a kind of sacrifice); on the sabbath the priests perform their functions in the temple without being accused of breaking the sabbath. If they can move about in the space of the temple, why can his disciples not do the same now in the space of the *new* temple, which is himself? Unexpected by the Pharisees, the reply is no less significant for us! Christ is replacing the old; he institutes a new order. What is the point of discussing the old?

Jesus adduces another argument, which is not from the Law, declared dead and defunct, but from the Prophets. He defines for them the will of God: mercy and not sacrifice (12:7; cf. Hos. 6:6; Amos 5:21). Jesus does not stray from the theme; he is not speaking of altar offerings but of the law of sabbath rest. He points out simply that God wants love more than ritual laws; human beings are more important than cultic "distractions." Because they did not understand this truth of God, the Pharisees condemned the guiltless (12:7). But were they not sinners? With his word, Jesus reversed the question, not with a subtle dialectic that silences the simple, but by exposing the false justice of the Pharisees. They will render account like genuine sinners for "not knowing" the salvific will of God and for condemning the innocent. This denunciation that Jesus directed against the judges of orthodoxy and orthopraxis provides much food for thought.

The second encounter occurs because of the presence of a paralytic in the synagogue, also on the sabbath day (12:9–14). It happens *before* the healing, a prelude which allows us to see the evil intention of those present who hasten to remind Jesus of the prohibition of work on the seventh day. They ask him if it is lawful to cure on the sabbath, not to learn something (the Pharisees know the Law) but to *accuse him* (12:10). In fact they know what Jesus will do. But Jesus is not deterred and he heals the sick person (12:13). His conscientizing reply to the intriguers must be set in bold relief here. He takes the example of a sheep that has fallen into a pit on the sabbath. But, most astutely, Jesus does not draw the example by reference to a third person; the Pharisees would have said that the Law had to be observed and the sheep left in the pit. Instead, he asks them what they would have done with their *own* sheep ("What man *of you*. . .?"). The "so it is lawful" of verse 12 presupposes acceptance of the argument. If such was the case, the lesson was administered: it is obvious that Jesus can heal on the sabbath. But the word of Jesus has an even greater impact when he remarks that in this particular instance *a human being,* and not an animal, is at issue. This Christ who makes the "human being" emerge in his Word and in his actions is most admirable. And in order to pursue this truth, he asserts that one can lawfully do good on the sabbath.

But Christ's miracle is not then left to later interpretation—which is given—but is accompanied by an illuminating and "critical" word. What a profound truth that it is not easy to conscientize the high and mighty! The Pharisees understood but did not "see" the truth. They were deliberately blind before the light. Even more, they vented their fury on Jesus and plotted to destroy him (12:14). His word had been "dangerous." It was dangerous to them—since it had penetrated their very souls—but they would later take it upon themselves to present it as dangerous to Caesar. It would be a way of "shifting" the accusation onto another plane where they could not be touched or discovered.

This gives rise to a question: is it worth the trouble to try to conscientize the oppressors on whatever plane they move? The light of the word of Jesus was illuminating, but the Pharisees retained only the denunciatory word: they did not change; their sin against the light became even more marked. For this reason Jesus will excoriate them later, pointing out to them their blasphemy against the Spirit. (We will see that John reinterprets this same passage with his symbol-laden language.)

In the third scene, with the demonized deaf mute (12:22–30), Jesus begins with the healing. This produces a twofold reaction: the multitude, *the people,* marvels and "interprets" the event as the sign of God's presence in Jesus: "Can this be the Son of David?" (12:23). On the other hand, the Pharisees are alarmed by this confession of faith in God, intentionally placed first in the structure of the account. Of the three actors (Jesus, the people, the Pharisees), the Pharisees stand apart and alone against the other two. The event was before them; it was the evidence.

But the Pharisees—the sapient ones, now utterly confused—need an "explanation." In the face of the truth—above all when it is grasped by the simple people—only the *lie* remains to them. They seize upon the lie that Jesus works in the name of the prince of the devils (12:24). And here Jesus' conscientizing word once more comes into play, pointing out to them the contradiction and the stupidity of the argument (12:24-30). At the same time, he teaches them that they are in the presence of a "sign of the times" (12:28) which they do not know enough to discern. In this way he connects his denunciation of their sin against the Spirit (12:31ff.) with his criticism of those who ask for a "sign" from heaven, a miracle to prove he was sent by God (12:38ff.). If the *presence* of Christ is the "sign" of the times what is the point of seeking other signs? But if they want another, it will not be a miracle for them, but the "sign" of the prophet Jonah: the people of Nineveh understood his message as the voice of God and were converted: ". . . and behold, something greater than Jonah is here" (12:41).

Matthew prolongs this "conscientization" through the word in many other passages. We shall dwell only on the discussion recorded in 15:1-20. Jesus is in Galilee and he is approached by Pharisees and scribes come from Jerusalem (a distance of approximately 170 kilometers) in order to ask him why his disciples do not wash their hands before eating. Ridiculous as this may appear, it has had innumerable parallels in the history of the Church, above all in religious customs—with their alienating structures and "control" from distant epicenters. The envoys came for wool and returned shorn. Jesus does not "explain" this freedom that he gave to his disciples, but he silences them with a counter-question to which they cannot reply and which exposes *them* as transgressors of the will of God. The example that bares their guilt refers precisely to the religious sphere, but it demonstrates that the religious "tradition" perverts a *human* value (15:4-6). Christ denounces sin where it dwells (in the Pharisees and not in his disciples) and he conscientizes about the will of God. Jesus quotes the prophets to further aggravate the bad conscience of his interlocutors, reminding them of inauthentic cult in its twofold dimension (see Chap. IV, Sec. 2).

The occurrences follow each other without respite. But let us leave the Synoptics to report on two word-deeds of Jesus, as recorded in the Gospel of John.

In the account of the Samaritan woman (John 4), there is an "encounter" between her and Jesus; it is at first superficial on her part but is subsequently deepened in truth. Let us reflect on the liberating pedagogy of the Master. The Jews "have no dealings" with the Samaritans (4:9). They relate according to generalized prejudices, not according to the value of particular persons. Jesus initiates the dialogue with her, thus accepting her as a person, regardless of her sins. The point of departure of all that follows is this opening to the person. With this "beginning" the conversation develops and Jesus will be able to require of her the whole truth, *her* truth (4:16ff.). What is important here is the result that Christ achieves: that *she* "say her word," that she manifest herself in her deepest being, which Jesus will complete by clarifying her confession (4:18). Her "sin" is pinpointed with exquisite fineness without condemning her. And because he does not condemn her, the dialogue continues until *she* takes another step forward and in Jesus discovers the Christ: "I know that Messiah is coming" (4:25ff.). This is a strange recognition for a Samaritan woman. She also spreads the news and many believe (4:39). What a dignity displayed by this woman, who up to that moment had been nothing! Christ had liberated her possibilities "to be more," to "say her word."

In the discussions that follow the healing of the man blind from birth (John 9), he also comes to "recognize" the Son of God (9:35ff.) from his own experience. Perhaps Christ approaches him again, after he is expelled from the synagogue, because of the correctness with which he had reflected on the author of his physical illumination: "If this man were not from God, he could do nothing" (9:33). This was the sign of a spiritual light that rendered him able to "believe." What, on the other hand, is the dialectic of the Pharisees? Their quibbles are various: "This man is not from God, for he does not keep the sabbath" (9:16); or perhaps he was not blind in the first place (9:18); "this man is a sinner" (9:24); "we are disciples of Moses; . . . as for this man we do not know where he comes from" (9:28ff.). All have a common denominator: the "religious" prejudice against Jesus because he heals a sick man on the sabbath (9:14). The facts recede in the background; the blind man whose sight was restored *must* be a "sinner" also because he thinks differently from them (9:34).

Jesus had said nothing to them up to this moment. Using the symbolism of light in relation to the cured blind man who came to believe, he asserts that he has come into the world for a "crisis," a "discernment" that turns things upside down: "that those who do not see may see, and that those who see may become blind" (9:39). The Pharisees pick up the allusion: "Are we also blind?" (9:40) and the Master subtly hits back at them again, turning the symbolism around: "If you were blind, you would have no guilt; but now that you say, 'We see,' your guilt *remains*" (9:41). On the one hand they are blind—and the whole scene reveals their inner darkness. However, if they themselves say that they "see" (the Pharisees "know" God; they know the truth like no other), that is their own condemnation. Unable to "see" from their "seeing," they have no way out. And their sin "remains." Christ at no time tries to change them. Thus the question raised previously poses itself anew: Is it possible to liberate oppressors *from within their own selves?* Does not the conscientizing word turn into a denunciation of sin? What did Christ accomplish with the Pharisees?

4. THE ANNOUNCEMENT TO THE POOR

The baptism in the Jordan was the prophetic manifestation of Jesus[3] and, as we saw above in section 1, a distant evocation of the Paschal mystery. Immediately thereafter he proclaims the advent of the "kingdom." But on the basis of his identification with the lowly and his behavior as the "suffering Servant," he can call the poor and the persecuted "blessed." These are the two lines of thought in the four original beatitudes, as recorded in Luke 6:20-23. (In Matthew 5:3-12 they are amplified with a more spiritual interpretation and another four of the same ethical tone are added.[4]) It is difficult to imagine that Jesus had proclaimed them at the beginning of his preaching, as Matthew 5:1ff. gives us to understand. They presuppose such a maturity in the disciples and such a self-understanding in Christ himself that it is best to situate them in the final phase of his public ministry. In a certain way, they allow us to glimpse the experience of the primitive Church of Jerusalem, poor and persecuted. If Matthew places them in their present position it is to emphasize their programmatic "meaning." They are the *proclamation* of Jesus, in other words, his essential message. The programmatic addresses made by chiefs of state upon their assumption of power are significant at the moment in which they are pronounced (although they are usually not carried out). But they are also valid with respect to the orientation they provide and the "possibilities" they reveal.

But if the evangelical beatitudes are also the *synthesis* of the preaching of Jesus, they acquire another importance. They are the result of his experience (the allusions to the persecutions of the Synagogue are indicative). They are particularly the result of his real commitment to the poor (he was truly poor himself, cf. Luke 9:58), and of his "service" to the brethren ("But I am among you as one who serves," Luke 22:27). His word, then, is based on *life.*

But do the beatitudes of Christ have anything to do with "liberation"? If those who are poor and persecuted for their ideal are "blessed," well then, let them continue being such. It would seem, in fact, that Jesus proclaims the resignation of the oppressed. The future kingdom of heaven will be theirs; they will be copiously compensated. More than once has the catechesis of the Church rendered this ill service to the Word of God! But this is not the way things are. To begin with, nothing tells us that the "kingdom of heaven" in the Gospels is a celestial and transcendent world, a post-mortem state. In the "story" of the rich gourmet and Lazarus there is no mention of the "kingdom" (Luke 16:19-31). We know how the Jews conceived of this "kingdom" for which they hoped, as earthly and very clearly defined.

The beatitudes must be read in the light of the messianic hopes inscribed in the heart of the prophets and elaborated by the Jews. There is a clear prophetic line in the Old Testament that takes up the theological conception of Yahweh as defender of the poor and ends in a description of the future king who will establish *justice* and liberate the oppressed (cf. Isa. 9:5-7; 11:1-9; Jer. 23:3-8; Ezek. 34:23-27). Let us consider the most significant passage for our purposes here: when Isaiah announces the scion of David, possessor of the "spirit" of Yahweh, he states that "with righteousness he shall judge *the poor,* and decide with equity for the *meek of the earth;* and he shall smite the earth with the rod of his mouth, and with the breath of his lips he shall slay the wicked" (Isa. 11:4).

Jesus "interprets" not only his vocation but also his historical moment as the realization of these hopes. "Blessed are the poor," because *now* with him liberation begins. The beatitudes are not a call to resignation but to a process of liberation; the process does not begin as a social and political revolution (we shall see why later), but sooner or later becomes one. If the "kingdom" is not the same ethereal, spiritual reality, then it will not arrive without a profound change in human beings, without the establishment of justice on all levels. We can interpret the beatitudes from the vantage point of the dominated world, which is on a structure of social "classes" (we believe that the concept of "Third World" is more ideological than "basic"). From this point of view the beatitudes are a summons to the oppressed to recognize the "signs of the times" and, full of hope, to set out on the long march to liberation. They are not a call to resignation but to a process of liberation.

We might wonder why Jesus did not express more clearly this thrust of his proclamation to the poor and persecuted. Moreover, the Gospel of Matthew bends this message in a spiritual and ethical direction. Indeed, the first Gospel is precisely a re-reading of the words of Jesus *from the vantage point* in which it was written (characterized by opposition between Christians and Pharisees). Our re-reading is made *from our own vantage point*. By recovering the core meaning of the evangelical kerygma, we understand it from a horizon that forces its surplus-of-meaning to emerge. The meaning of an expression is always "reduced" by the context in which it is spoken or written. But the distance of that context permits us to re-open that meaning and broaden its first horizon of expression. What Matthew did in one direction, we can do in another, inasmuch as we are situated in another context of appropriation of the original meaning. Thus the re-reading goes further— toward us rather than away from us, because it is "in front" of the text—than the meaning offered by the author of a text. Indeed, it is an act of exploration, the only way of surpassing the "history" of the meaning and of fruitfully appropriating it for oneself. This is the path traversed by the hermeneutical act, to the discussion of which we shall return.

5. THE "LIBERATING" DEATH OF JESUS

The Gospels signal a Jewish moment and a Roman moment in the trial of Jesus. The first is not purely religious, since the Sanhedrin also enjoyed a political power. Let us recall that the Roman procurator resided in Caesarea, a strategic point no doubt, but one distant from the epicenter of Jewish institutional life, which was Jerusalem. Under the cover of religion, the Sanhedrin played a political role within the framework of a theocratic worldview. From the time of the post-exilic restoration the high priest concentrated political as well as religious power in his hands, limited only by the overlords who successively ruled over the Jews—the Romans at this particular time.

The key for understanding the trial of Jesus is not Pilate, but the Sanhedrin. Throughout the Gospel narratives, nothing occurs that might have alarmed the Romans, but much occurs that disturbs the Jews and leads to the denouncement that we know. We must read the passion account situated within the structure of the whole Gospel; this is the minimum that can be demanded from the interpreter. We have seen that the actions and the words of Jesus—geared toward the recovery of the essential human being and natural human values—stirred up rage on the part of the power-wielding groups (high priests, elders, scribes, Pharisees) and led to the decision to eliminate him. The praxis of Jesus (action and theory in mutual interdependence) unmasked the superstructural and ideological universe controlled by the leaders of Israel, and whose axis of support was the Law understood as "tradition."

Thus Jesus' praxis becomes "critical" and infuriating, immediately becoming part of the fatal circle of the "power" question. This is made explicit precisely in the transition from the public activity of Jesus to his arrest and delivery into the hands of the Jerusalem authorities (seek Mark 11:27ff.; Matt. 21:23; Luke 20:1ff.). The high priests, the scribes, and the elders (they are the instances of power, not religious factions!) interrogate him: "*By what authority are you doing these things?*" The scenes that follow (Mark 12 and parallels: the parable of the *homicidal* vine-dressers, the tribute to Caesar, the question of the Messiah, etc.) depict a Jesus who is a rival to the authority and the distorted mission of the Jewish leaders, who want to liquidate him but who are restrained by their fear of the people (Mark 11:18; 12:12; 14:1-2).

The trial of Jesus begins before the Sanhedrin (Mark 14:53ff.), where the "proofs" that lead to his death sentence are hatched. We shall not dwell on what is already well known; we underscore merely that Jesus appears as *subversive to the religious order.*

What are the specific charges against him in his trial? First, his assertion that he can destroy the temple (the house of God!) (Matt. 26:61, 27:40). It is not a charge brought by false witnesses, who turn out to be worthless (26:59-60). Rather, two final witnesses come forward and report what they have heard; indeed the evangelists elsewhere corroborate this testimony (cf. John 2:19). In the second place, he is accused of having called himself the Son of God, which does not signify the divine person of the Son but rather the Messiah (Matt. 26:63; John 19:7). Scandalized by the messianic confession of Jesus (Mark 14:61ff.), the high priest tears his robes. For the high priest, the religious realm here touched on the political. The Messiah would be the savior of the Jews, but the leaders of Israel could not bear the thought that *he* should be the liberator, he who had so tellingly challenged their privileges and power. But by such conduct they quickly exposed themselves as collaborators of the dominant power.

At that time the Jews could not on their own authority carry out a death sentence; only the Romans enjoyed the *jus gladii,* or the right to apply capital punishment. The intention to "liquidate" Jesus, manifested so many times (Matt. 12:14; John 5:18; 7:1, 25, 44ff.; 8:37; 10:31; etc.) had to be implemented at the civil level and on grounds of "state security." This is why they brought him before Pilate (Mark 15:1). Before the Roman procurator they could adduce only a *political* charge, related to subversion against the new order of domination. Thanks to its religious-political ambiguity, the figure of the "Messiah" conveniently lends itself to an attack on Jesus on two fronts: in the religious order he was judged as a blasphemer for calling himself the Christ, the son of God; in the political order, it signified a pretention to usurp the power held by the Romans. Consequently, it was not difficult to transfer the trial from the Sanhedrin to the Roman jurisdiction. Pilate's question ("Are you the King of Jews?") shows that he was well-informed: Jesus was one more case of a would-be liberator from the domination that Pilate represented and maintained.

Mark is very generic and indefinite in regard to the charges against Jesus: "They. . . delivered him to Pilate" (15:1); "and the chief priests accused him of many things" (15:3; cf. 15:4); to the question "what evil has he done?" Mark has the crowds give no answer (15:4). But Luke is explicit and points up the transition. The religious trial that condemns him for blasphemy is succinctly described in 22:66-71. As soon as it is over his judges go to Pilate and make *other* charges against him: "We found this man *perverting* our *nation,* and forbidding us to give tribute to Caesar, and saying that he himself is the *King* Messiah" (23:1-2). Notable here is the attribute of "king" that is emphatically associated with the Messiah. (In 22:70ff., on the other hand, what mattered to his religious judges was to catch him in blasphemy for having called himself the "Son of God," even though that title too referred to the Messiah.) The mention of "king" was bound to alarm the Roman functionary, so the Jewish authorities contrived a "political crime" in order to ensure the success of their designs.

Luke, like the other Synoptics, had already described the scene of the tribute to Caesar (20:19-26), in which Jesus marked out the political and religious areas in question. But the main point here, as the evangelists note, is that the scribes and priests do not question him in order to learn for themselves at first hand—a negative reply would have made it possible to bring charges against him. Instead they "sent spies, who pretended to be sincere, that they might take hold of what he said, *so as to deliver him* to the authority and jurisdiction of the governor" (20:20). In his preaching Jesus may have alluded to the liberation of the Jewish people—the whole prophetic line signalled this liberation —but the tribute scene purposes to show the evil intentions of his co-religionists; they are discredited, since the reply of the Lord seems to remind them that they do not give to God the things that are God's.

Pilate's intuition is noteworthy. He does not lose his calm despite the charge of "subversive" hurled against Jesus—and repeated later; "He *stirs up the people*" (Luke 23:5)—and despite Christ's own acknowledgement that he was "King of the Jews": "You have said so " (23:3). Indeed, he replies: "I find no crime in this man" (23:4). And after Herod's disappointed interrogation, the governor's suspicion is again confirmed: "you brought me this man as one who was *perverting the people;* and after examining him before you, behold, I did not find this man guilty of any of your charges against him" (23:14). He insists on his innocence three times (23:20, 22).

All four evangelists note the effort of the Roman governor to free Jesus, but John is the one who lays greatest stress (after Luke) on Pilate's conviction that Jesus was innocent and on his attempts to negotiate his release. We are accustomed to a denigration of Pilate because he delivered Christ to his executioners even though he knew him to be innocent. That weakness is obvious. But we do not carefully consider all that he did to save Jesus and the pressures playing on him that forced him to go contrary to his knowledge and conscience: "If this man were not an evildoer, we would not have handed him over" (John 18:30); "If you release this man, you are not Caesar's friend; every one who makes himself a king sets himself against Caesar" (19:12); "We have no king but Caesar" (19:15). And recall the thousand voices that shouted down the order of Jesus' release.

Despite this play of orchestrated pressures, Pilate ventures, as a last pressing argument, to present Jesus as the "king of the Jews" (19:14). It is possible, moreover, to read the Greek text of 19:13 as stating that Pilate sat *Jesus* in the judge's seat, the symbol of his royalty.[5] This would be in accord with the words of presentation—"Here is your King!" (19:14)—and with the Johannine theology of "judgment" that *Christ* pronounces on the Jews, a theme that courses throughout the fourth Gospel. John is the only one also to narrate the episode of the inscription on the cross: "Jesus of Nazareth, *King of the Jews*." The chief priests protest it because it was tantamount to saying that Jesus was right: "Do not write . . . , but, '*This man* said, I am King of the Jews.' " We know Pilate's lapidary reply: "What I have written, I have written" (19:22). Obviously, he wishes to say that Christ was right, even postmortem. One truth *remains* established in John's perspective: Christ is the *true King* of the Jews.

Another evaluation of Pilate is called for. On two occasions Christ tells him "his" truth (John 18:36ff.; 19:11). The Roman grasps Jesus' transcendent mission better than did the Jews. Thus he does not fear to proclaim his "regal" dignity, which he knows does not offend that of Caesar. Once more we are confirmed in our notion that the political charge against Jesus was an excuse; that the Pharisees had to do away with this prophet who was denouncing them for their sinful "not-knowing" the God manifested in him.

No less important is it to note that it was the *power-wielders*—in this case the *religious* hierarchy—who plotted against Jesus. During the whole course of his public ministry, *the people* marvelled at Jesus' doctrine, to the point that they recognized that he was speaking with greater authority (because he was speaking from *life*) than their scribes and priests (Mark 1:22-27). The people are always more open to the truth. The structures are closed to anything new and pervert its meaning. Moreover, the Gospels note that it is the religious chiefs of Jerusalem who lead the hostility, the denigration, and the trial against Jesus. This is in line with prophetic accusation against this city which is precisely the one that killed the prophets (cf. Luke 13:34f.). This phenomenon has been repeated so many times (in the Church!).

At Jesus' trial it is the religious authorities, clearly identified, who stage-manage the great lie of history. They are the chief accusers (Luke 23:10). We Christians have been ingenuous, at times, in blaming the Jewish *people,* charging that they made an "about-face," betraying Jesus after his triumphal reception in Jerusalem. The intrigue came from the religious authorities. If the people were present, we must note two things: first, we do not know how large a segment of it (the *people* as such is not easily deceived, because of its marvelous grasp of the truth); second, the collaborationist group had been "bought" (and thus it could not be the whole people) by the chief priests and the elders who "*pursuaded* the people to ask for Barabbas and *destroy Jesus*" (Matt. 27:20).[6]

We can add a few observations. Some scholars believe that Mark presents an original account and that Luke distorts the trial of Jesus.[7] It does seem that Luke adds and completes where Mark synthesizes. However, on reading the account of the trial before Pilate in Mark one does get the impression of a spotty and abridged presentation. What is registered in Luke seems more coherent, with a political sentence that is a sophisticated consequence of a *religious* trial (with political connotations!) and that is eminently intelligible within the framework of the Jewish universe of that time. There must have been something very serious behind Pilate's calm and composure before one accused of sedition, of subversion against Caesar, of presenting himself as a candidate for the kingship of the Jews. He must have been sufficiently shrewd to perceive the real question at issue.

On the other hand, I believe that it is overly imaginative to assert that the Gospels do not wish to blame the Romans for the death of Jesus, thus strengthening the charge against the Jews with the aim of obtaining a "captatio benevolentiae" for preaching the Gospel in the empire. If such were the case the Gospels would have attributed a more lucid judgment to the Roman procurator. John, for his part, writes when the imperial persecutions against the Christian communities were already increasing in intensity. It is the time of the Apocalypse! Rather, the entire trial of Jesus has its epicenter in the Jewish leaders of Jerusalem: elders, scribes, priests, and the religious groups.

One paradox, previously introduced, remains: Why did the Jewish authorities not exploit the new leader in order to assert the hope of liberation from the Roman yoke? That is the question. On the one hand, Jesus by degrees is undermining the symbolic world that sustains their power, that is, the law, tradition, "authority," the privilege that sets them above others—all of which conditioned a real oppression of consciences and of human values. Christ unmasks the oppressors and liberates the oppressed. On the other hand, the hierarchs of Jerusalem are "in good" with the Romans. The latter dominate Palestine, bleeding it white with onerous tributes, but they permit a certain internal autonomy in government, with local theocratic chiefs. The latter *owe* their posts and titles to Caesar. Thus they collaborate with Rome and betray their people. The presence of a "Messiah" complicated their status. There was no better way out than to petition Caesar for help against this imposter and subversive!

Was Jesus a revolutionary? What did he teach the Jews to liberate them from Roman domination? To answer that question, and to discover a "political Christ," many have embraced the idea that Jesus belonged to the Zealot group, revolutionaries who directly and violently attacked Rome's intervention. The presentation of this question by Cullmann and others is already classic.[8] Truth to tell, there is not much evidence in favor of a pro-Zealot Jesus. Those who try thus to identify him do not realize that they are doing a disservice to the cause of liberation. The Zealots, actually, were reactionary groups. If they pursued the goal of expelling the Romans from Palestinian soil, it was to re-establish the Law and the lost politico-religious institutions. They could not get out of the "infernal circle" of legalism.[9] Christ could not struggle or die for the law; rather, he suffered its power as a structure of death. To long for a Zealot Christ, therefore, is to follow a reactionary, religio-nationalistic Christ. Recovering one's particular religious and cultural values is one thing; recovering an oppressive legal system is another. Jesus came to save people, not the law.

We are of the opinion that the question of Christ as "liberator" must be expressed in a different manner. Let us understand each other: this Christ is not only the Christ of eschatology or the Christ of a purely spiritual or mystical understanding of liberation. Christians committed *to real human beings* continue to ponder the political, socio-economic, and cultural implications of the religious message of Jesus, rather than ambiguous themes such as "reconciliation in Christ" (whose theological profundity remain concealed through an ideological use of it in preaching).[10]

The message of Jesus does not appear as a program, much less as a strategy of political liberation. He was a religious leader. The Zealots were religious revolutionaries who wanted a return to tradition through the expulsion by fire and sword of the pagan Roman overlords. Jesus, on the other hand, did nothing to liberate the Jews from the Roman yoke. It is as if he had not come to the political and nationalist commitment of the Zealots. Nonetheless, precisely therein lies his lucidity and his greatness. Had he been a revolutionary leader he would have helped *the Jews* on the surface, and his activity would have exhausted itself on that political, racial, and geographical level. Let us recall that the Exodus was a symbol of liberation over the centuries, but only for the people *of Israel*. Only from the time of Christ was this symbol universalized. There are also other elements that come into consideration.

The actions of Jesus do have a political dimension—though in a universal sense; they provide the indirect but indispensable foundation for a radical liberation, one under another sign. We must proceed methodologically in order to understand this more clearly. On the one hand, we must discern the implications of the practices of Jesus; on the other hand, we cannot avoid a hermeneutical consideration that critically elucidates our access to the gospel texts that speak of Jesus. Hence the two points that follow:

1. If Jesus had been in the first instance a political revolutionary, either in

the Zealot manner or—as a possibility—by surpassing the *religious-nationalist* mode, the meaning of his action would have exhausted itself within the Jewish horizon. *At that time* his actions would not have unleashed a liberation theology for other races or peoples. The italicized words serve to distinguish Jesus' situation from that of the Exodus or from our own. Jesus' situation must be distinguished from that of Exodus, because here the *new* event could engender an original symbolics and an unprecedented historical consciousness. It must be distinguished from our own inasmuch as the scientific and critical analysis of reality (peculiar to modernity) permits the believer to discern a kerygmatic and theological significance in a revolutionary *political* action. *At that time,* on the other hand, the religious conceptions of the Jews, centered on the cult of the law and on the ideology of "election," would have presented these two possibilities of reading the revolutionary event.

Let us consider, on the other hand, that the play of contradictions of the different groups could not be made to come together. Although the Zealots radically opposed the Romans—and thus represented the principal contradiction—the Sadducees did not even feel the imperial oppression, for it was to the imperial representatives that they owed their posts and their "authority" over the oppressed people. Given such a state of affairs, one feels that Jesus is closer to the Zealots than to the other "religious" people who, in fact, were traitors to the people. But this principal Roman-Jewish contradiction, sustained by the Zealots, undoubtedly would have emerged as a new contradiction between an oppressive law and a people oppressed by Jewish structures and traditions, now allowed to flourish with their own ideological and juridical force. And nothing would have been done for the sake of *human beings.*

Accordingly Jesus had to move in another direction. His actions, in the first place, shifted from the law to human beings. What matters, after all, is not the salvation of the Jews so that they can freely live according to the law, but liberation from *every structure of death* and the reclaiming of the human being. Jesus began a new process of liberation by enlightening the consciousness oppressed by religious ideology. In the second place, Jesus establishes a new praxis, whose axis is service to and love of the other. This praxis is bound to put on guard the power-wielders, who have much to do with any oppression or domination. Love of neighbor becomes political practice. The first case is that of Jesus himself: for having initiated and proclaimed a praxis of conscientization and salvation, he drew upon himself all the ire of the Jewish authorities, more than that of the Romans, and perhaps even the displeasure of the Zealots. We have already commented on this.

It sufficed for Jesus, therefore, to initiate his program of liberation by *redeeming human beings* from the structural power of the law, of "traditions," and of the marginalizing prejudices. He denounces the "justice of the law" in the Pharisees (see especially Matthew, and Paul's theological elaboration) and the perverted and alienating "authority" of the Sadducees. Obviously it will be the authority, and not the Pharisees, who later will orchestrate the trial and the execution of the new leader of the Palestinian people.[11]

As a leader, Jesus generates a new symbolical order that culminates in the political sphere.[12] Insofar as the *poor* are conscientized, they become a new force. They will be the basis of the primitive church and a decisive factor in the weakening of the Roman Empire. Equality among all people will produce a rupture within the socioeconomic system of the ancient world: the slaves of the empire will be the revolutionary ferment of the first centuries of the Christian faith. The cult of the emperor-god crumbles at the roots and is demythologized on all levels, thus losing its oppressive function sustained by the mythical ideology. The anthropological, and not the Jewish-nationalist, thrust of the praxis of Jesus universalizes it. Through union with the other elements indicated above it can generate processes of liberation of the whole person in any nation or human group. The synthesis lies in that capacity of the deeds and the words of Christ to liberate *human beings* from every alienating and oppressive system, whether religious or political. Consequently any justification of some purely "spiritual mission" of the churches and of Christians is inane. If Jesus' mission had been only "spiritual," he would not have met the fate that was his.

2. Christian history instructs us that the gospel kerygma is ambiguous. We rightly lament the many instances of a return to a theocratic worldview, of a withdrawal into the "spiritual" realm, of collaboration with the dominant groups. There has been a resistance to accompany the liberation processes as far as our "speeches" go—such as those delivered at Medellín[13] during the Second General Conference of Latin American Bishops.

It happens that theology lacks a *hermeneutical* elaboration of the Gospel. To what measure is the Gospel sufficient as an indicator for present-day Christian praxis? In the symbolical order engendered by Christ, which we have already noted, we find a key to the interpretation of our faith for the purpose of making a contribution to the liberation of our peoples.

But there is something left unsaid in the Gospel: the political, socioeconomic, and cultural dimension of the task of the Christian and of the churches. On the one hand, the *reality* that we live is different from that of the Jews of the Palestine of Jesus; on the other hand, our possibilities of "reading" this reality are different and arouse another type of *conscientization*. The advent of the social sciences cannot supplant the Gospel; the two are on different levels. But the social sciences help us to discover in the Gospel a reservoir-of-meaning that emerges only in the perspective of our own situation. Thus appears what was left "unsaid" by the biblical kerygma. The meaning of Christ's praxis is codified in a *text* which, as linguistic structure and as a message, has a "before," an "in front of," that is open to interpretation. This is not something *added* to the original meaning. It is this same meaning read in a more inclusive and richer dimension. The trial of Jesus then becomes newly illuminating, because it is newly illuminated. This is one way of describing the task facing biblical hermeneutics.[14]

6. CHRIST AND THE LAW

This theme seems peculiar to Pauline theology (see the following chapter). Paul meditates from a special angle, that of the "mystery" of the death-resurrection, with all its implications. We shall see this. The Gospels, on the other hand, spotlight Jesus' *attitudes* toward the Law, the concrete institutions that represented it, his conscientizing Word, and his final trial in the name of his fidelity to the prophetic vocation. This historical Jesus (not only the paschal Christ) has a tremendous significance.

Why did the *religious authorities* of Jerusalem condemn Jesus?

We are in the presence of a paradox pregnant with mystery. Religious truth, when it loses its focus, is the greatest source of human alienation; power, when it is perverted, is the typical symbol of oppression. Religious power, when it loses sight of the God of the event, is the most tyrannical. It has spiritual weapons at its disposal, and, at its peak, it has even taken recourse to material weapons (not necessarily civil power, as in the trial of Jesus and on other occasions, but also to intrigue, suspension from teaching posts, etc.).

The Law implies an innate tendency to death for the very reason that it also gives life: as an expression of the divine will, human beings observe it in order *to be faithful* to God. But God manifests himself in new events that must be "gathered up" hermeneutically in a new law. The Covenant of Sinai had issued forth from the salvific experience of the Exodus. The precept of love given by Jesus at the last supper is not arbitrary or intellectually deduced from a definition of God. Rather, it is endorsed by the liberating gesture of Christ who *delivers himself* up to death for the cause of humanity. The commandment of love should culminate in an equal gesture: it must lead to "death" for others. There will be different forms and gradations, but the demand is clear, as is seen in its first witness. Nevertheless religious people frequently close themselves off in the law-structure, which quite easily omits love or contradicts it in the testimony to others. From this moment on, it has lost its "theo-logical" sense; it no longer "talks of God."

We must reflect deeply on that saying of Jesus: "Think not that I have come to abolish the law and the prophets; I have come not to abolish them but to fulfull them" (Matt. 5:17). How does he "fulfill" the Law by unmasking its utilization for oppression and by "freeing" his disciples from its observance? How does he "fulfill" the Law if they kill him on account of it and for transgressing it? How does he "fulfill" it, finally, if it is not subsumed in the New Alliance and if Christ never speaks of new structures for the new people of God? In reality, Jesus fulfills the Law insofar as he "consummates" it, brings it to its end, and, by the same token, annuls it (the notion of "consummation," or *teleiosis*). Jesus, as the new event of God in the world, *exhausts* the deep meaning of the Law *in love*. Without promulgating laws, he recovers in love the reservoir-of-meaning of the Law, understood originally as a path of life, as an interpretation of the liberation event of the Exodus.

The conscientizing attitudes of Christ have their significance, as we see. The "sabbath" was the touchstone of the legalistic mentality of the Pharisees. And it is precisely the "sabbath"—the day of the "memory" of the liberation—that is disregarded by Christ, because it had paradoxically become a source of alienations and the oppression of consciences. Until recently the same was true of the "Sunday" obligation in the Christian church. We all remember the moral conflicts uselessly provoked by juridical teaching. The change in attitude toward this and so many other ecclesiastical laws is not due to a loss of the meaning of sin (a loss that represents another kind of "alienation") but rather to a greater commitment to the world. It is part of the process of liberation in which Christ educated his genuine disciples.

Christ "consummates" the Law and "gathers up" its salvific sense in love. That is the program that he offers Christians. On the basis of that "liberation" we can enter more joyfully into the process of the "liberation" of our brothers and sisters.

CHAPTER VI

Paul: Radical Human "Liberation"

In the deepest stratum of New Testament theology we find the theme of salvation through *faith in Christ*. What does this have to do with "liberation"? Much, to be sure. Faith in Christ means recognizing that God has spoken through him, through his life and his word, through his death and his resurrection. It means that he is the salvation event that must be "gathered up" into any kerygmatic confession and expressed in a new life. Christ did not tell his disciples before-hand how they were to interpret events and problems. God manifests himself *in the events* themselves. But the Christ event, in its totality, was the new light for discovering the will of God. The new light was given by the Spirit, who is always the gift of the Risen One.

The events of the council of Jerusalem—focused on the problem of the Law for neophytes—are a model of interpretation of the "signs of the times." Note the words of Peter, which are a hermeneutical interpretation of two earlier "manifestations" of the Spirit (Acts 15:7-11 in connection with 2:1ff. and 10:34ff.). The Church must "understand" Christ in light of his new epiphanies in history (note the hermeneutical key given in John 16:12-15) and through the praxis of love. Christ will "manifest" himself to those who love, according to the same Gospel of John (14:21).

Faith in Christ liberates from all that is not a manifestation of the true countenance of God. Faith gives us the full "truth," a truth that "makes us free" because it is the light of a Word-event (John 8:32) that has nothing to do with the structures of the pagan-cosmic or Jewish-legalist world.

Here we connect with Paul who, in his letter to the Romans tells us that in Christ the full "justice" of God (a salvific, not a juridical expression) manifests itself through the openness of faith in the Risen One (3:21f., in the light of 1:16-17).

Paul condenses his kerygmatic theology into the saving event of the death-resurrection of Christ. All the epistles attest to it. But what we want to demonstrate now is his understanding and expression of the paschal mystery in "liberation" categories. Later, we shall point up the heremeneutical implications of this.

The meaning of Christ's death-resurrection as a liberation event is discussed by Paul in the central section of the letter to the Romans (3:21-8:3). This passage is set in bold relief by the synthesis of the negative pagan and Jewish experience (1:18-3:20): "All have sinned and fall short of the 'glory' [salvific epiphany] of God" (3:23). The great Pauline affirmation is this: *Christ liberates us from death, from Law, and from sin.* Why does he use the language of "liberation"? Why those three terms (Law, sin, death) and not others? How are they linked with each other and how do they explain each other? The light shed by this point of departure will enable us to understand this message existentially from the perspective of our Latin American reality.

For clarity's sake we shall try to break down the units of meaning into their component parts and, subsequently, recombine them in a connected whole.

1. THE TRIPLE ALIENATION

The paschal mystery is a liberation from death, from the Law, and from sin, for these three realities "estrange" us from our proper being, from our vocational possibilities. How does this alienation occur?

Sin. Adam's sin expresses the pride of human beings who long to appropriate for themselves the divine, to possess infinite and autonomous "knowledge." Indeed, this is how sin "came into the world," according to Romans 4:12; the myth of Adam expresses as an archetypical "event" that which is an "occurrence" in every person; the explication of what already "exists" in the world, as we shall see. In the biblical kerygma "sin" first of all sets itself against faith, rather than love; the latter results from the former in the experience of salvation. Recall the gamut of faith to which we alluded earlier: faith as "recognition" of God, as "trust" in his Word, as "fidelity" to the Covenant, as "acceptance" of the emissary, as "openness" to the gift, and as "strength" in witness. The Bible likewise offers us an inverse spectrum of sin as "not knowing" God, "mistrust," "infidelity," "denial" of God's mediations, "closure" to the gift, "weakness" in temptation. In faith at its peak, of course, there is love of God encountered in salvific events, a love that is extended as love of others. At the peak of non-faith, on the other hand, there is sin as non-love, the gesture of non-recognition of God and of the other, of closing off.

Thus sin is the maximal expression of *egoism*. They mutually define each other. Their equivalent is alienation. Sin-egoism is alienation in a double sense. First, by dislocating human beings vis-à-vis themselves, it produces a "vacuum-of-being"; they "are less" in the language of Freire; they are "liars" in that of John (8:44, 55). Egoism is infinite desire for what is beyond limits (the "divine"); it loses sight of the infinite demand (of love) in finitude. Second, sin-egoism closes up human beings within themselves and does not permit them to give of themselves. Thus, it blocks their most intimate vocation. Instead of enriching themselves with the "poverty" of the gift (2 Cor. 8:9), they impoverish themselves by "hoarding up" their non-gift.

Thus, human beings attempt, through a new alienation, to cover their "being less" by a "having more" that they take from others. They are oppressed by their own web that entangles and suffocates. Others are oppressed by a "having less" and, especially, by "being less" that originates in the egoism of the oppressor, not in their own will. We have deliberately shifted the question, from sin-egoism in general to sin-egoism in a socioeconomic sense. The relation between them is very deep-seated. We stress that the situations of alienating "dependence" in which many peoples or groups live have their subterranean root in this singular human capacity for "concentration" or "auto-centration" on the effective level: as will to power, to "know," to possess merit, or to "have."

Death. Our greatest consciousness of "limits" comes to us from the certainty that ultimately death awaits us. This "being-for-death" is a source of anguish—a theme copiously discussed in existentialism. Our "existential decision" may "pro-ject" us creatively into the world as "being-there"; or we may know that we will continue in our descendants (an idea expressed in religions and in social utopias that is also common in the subsconscious); or we may discover God in events and become committed to them. But in all cases we picture death as an insurmountable limit where we must "step down" and give up everything. Thus Adam's "infinite desire" did not consist only of a hankering to "know" like God; he wanted also to "be" like God and not die. The serpent, symbol of desire-seduction, explains to the woman: "You will not die. For God knows that when you eat of it your eyes will be opened, and *you will be like God,* knowing good and evil" (Gen. 3:4). The gods are fundamentally defined by their infinite knowledge and their immortality, science and life that constitute the basis of their supereminent "power."

Summing up, death frustrates the human desire for total self-realization. Could there be "liberation" from death, thus understood, without a new ontological pride.

What we have just unfolded in the limit-consciousness of death has its reverberations in the experience of oppression. By nullifying the oppressed, by rendering them "less," and by impeding their historical self-realization, the oppressors *hasten their death.* The history of the exploitation of our peoples and of the entire Third World is darkened by happenings that anticipate the destiny-of-death by a destiny-to-death in life.

The Law. The Law of the Covenant of Mount Sinai—or its subsequent "re-readings"—was an expression of the commitment to God and neighbor that emerged from the experience of the liberation from the bondage in Egypt: "You have *seen* what I did . . ." (Exod. 19:4; cf. in Deut. 29:1ff., and Josh. 23:3, the exhortations that extended other alliances). The book of Deuteronomy, like Psalm 119, is a beautiful poem on the Law as the way to the plenitude of salvation or as a mark of the just before God.

Nevertheless, the values of the Law are inverted the moment it moves out of the orbit of life and, consequently, humankind. This happens for three reasons. In the first place the law points to *exteriority,* to that which comes from outside us and which we must take into account in every action. The law is "given" to me; I receive it and I cannot even opt not to accept it without "punishment." Behind my transgression looms the shadow of the Judge and the punishment with which I must expiate the offense.

In the second place, it is *un-creative.* It can orientate and show the "way" when it is *a message* and signals a "vocation" that can be realized through personal options not already marked out by its tracks in advance. But the law-structure, in the civil and religious spheres, blocks creativity, to which is anticipated the "already-said" of the regulation. The law is un-creative from another negative perspective as well. A prescription is not observed infinitely, but only up to its proper "limit." This boundary also signals my "righteousness." The demand of justice or of love as enjoined by the prophets, on the other hand, is infinite. In the latter case even sin will be of a radical character instead of being "measured" by the limit of the law.

In the third place, law becomes *gnosis:* I am just because I fulfill the law that I "know." The Pharisees save themselves because they "know" the Law. Those who are ignorant of it are condemned. The pharisaic consciousness that Christ criticized so frequently and the alienation peculiar to it that Paul was to explore later is in the final analysis of *gnostic consciousness.* We are not speaking of the self-knowledge of later Gnosis (though it too could degenerate into "self-glorification"), but of a "gnosis" sufficient unto itself that includes a practice that is "justifying" by definition. The Law presents itself as a totalization of the will of God (although all Law, or *Torah* is revelation, more important is the notion that all revelation is *Torah*). But since the Law enters into an equation between "instruction" (*Torah!*) and obedience, the gnosis-practice of the Law becomes an infallible criterion of "righteousness" and of merit.

The Pharisees are saved from the very moment—and then because—they fulfill the Law. They declare their own righteousness, measured by their observance of the norm whose "limit" they possess cognitively. They simply cannot be "sinners." They are only "just." To them applies the parable of the publican who needs the mercy of God and the Pharisee who smugly confesses only his "merits" to God. Christ's saying, "For I came not to call the 'righteous,' but sinners" (Matt. 9:13) likewise is directed to the Pharisee. What is most grievous in pharisaism is that its interpretation of the Law empties it of love of God. The sinners, in their humility, asks for the mercy of God and therefore they *love God more.* "He who is forgiven little, loves little," says Luke (7:47), in a subtle allusion to the Pharisee present who observed the law but could not love like the sinful woman; not knowing how to love, he performed none of the kind acts, not prescribed by the Law, with which she had welcomed Jesus.

Later, Paul will explain to us why the Pharisees have no need of Christ. We see that the Law, interpreted as a self-justifying "gnosis," is the source of human alienation. Indeed, if the practice of the commandment is *my* work, if I justify *myself* in it without needing God to expound it to me (I "know" it through the "limit" that the Law determines), of what particular use is this Law to me and this praxis in the void? Is it not a form of self-oppression, a very curious one, to be sure? Can God be in it, at the same time he is "removed" by the very self-sufficiency of that gnosis-praxis? Was not this paradox of self-alienation through the Rule-praxis repeated exactly in the Church's religious life, oppressed by juridicism and its claim to "measure" and classify the will of God?

The Law is oppressive from still another angle, that of the "delicate and scrupulous conscience" of the Pharisee (or, often, of the Christian), according to the formula of Paul Ricoeur, whose analysis we shall summarize here in a few lines.[1] Such a conscience is heteronomous to the extreme: we obey in everything, all aspects included, in spite of everything, and down to each and every detail. It is a happy conscience because it is accepted (and in this it is still not alienated). Nevertheless, if *doing* the will of God, thus understood, is of greatest import, then it is a blessing to have the Law and, along with it, opportunities to *fulfill* it and to acquire merits. And here that self-oppression in the void, mentioned above, reappears. Moreover, the Pharisees are subjected to the judicial, definitional, and legislative activity of the rabbis and scribes; to this they must adjust their own "gnosis" of the Law without any possibility of deciding or of "saying their own word." To this "juridicization" of praxis is added a tendency to the ritualization of ethics (a legal exactitude parallel to that of the ritual), to sedimentation (more and more precepts are added) and to separation (the Pharisees are "separated"—such is the etymology of the word) from the "ignorant and sinners."

Lastly, the failure of this scrupulous and compliant conscience is *hypocrisy*. Why? Because the addition of ever more commandments makes their observance a superhuman feat and thus the "doing" masks itself in the "saying": "For they preach, but do not practice" (Matt. 23:3). The Law becomes a yoke. The Pharisees cannot break out of this fatidic circle that alienates them ever more. What is particularly sad is that the Pharisees cannot liberate themselves because they are oppressors of their own selfhood.

2. THE THREE ALIENATIONS, ACCORDING TO ROMANS 5-7

We have tried to understand the locus of the alienation of sin, death, and the Law, the three terms that Paul uses in his letter to the Romans. How do they relate to each other and "speak" to each other in the author's thought? The first reality that "comes into" the world is sin (*hamartia*, cf. 5:12). If in Adam there is a personal disobedience to the divine command (a *parabasis, parakoe,* 5:14ff.), the same is not said of his descendants. Since Adam *hamartia* has "reigned" in the world (5:21). It "was" (5:13), but it was "not counted" (*ouk eliogeitai*, 5:13). In v. 14 a distinction is made between Adam and "those whose sins were not like the transgression of Adam." Nevertheless, *hamartia* is a tremendous reality that "dwells within me" (7:20); through Adam's disobedience many (all) "were made sinners" (*katestathesan,* 5:19). This is an element for deducing the presence in the world of a "situational sin" that, nevertheless, is not personal sin. In what fashion, through what "occasion" will it become such?

In the second place, Paul establishes the reality of *death,* which also "reigns" in the world (5:14, 17) into which it came *through the sin* of Adam (5:12; cf. 5:15-17). This is a causal sequence: from sin to death. In making the Adam-Christ typology (5:15-19), Paul points out three consequences of the disobedience of the protogenitor:

—Many died (5:15), but grace and the gift of Jesus Christ are "much more." In v. 17 *life* is set over against death with even greater clarity.

—There is a condemnation (*katakrima*) for all. It is understood that this is a condemnation to death, as we see by the contrast, which established righteousness *(dikaioma)* for life (5:16, 18).

—Many were made sinners; through Christ many will be made righteous (5:19).

The sin-death relationship is both complicated and clarified by the position of the Law, the third element decisive in every respect. Paul is explicit on this point. The first consequence of the coming of the Law is the transmutation of sin (*hamartia*) from being an excusable transgression to an *imputable* one (5:13). Sin, therefore, is different before and after the bestowal of the Law. It is no longer situational, but personal. It is no longer the sin of the world, but is appropriated as guilt. In what manner does this come about?

Throughout his exposition (5-8) Paul again takes up and explains his assertion of 3:20, which is the last verse of the antithetical section on the time (not chronological but existential) of the wrath of God. The Law, far from being able to justify, shows its intrinsic weakness since it gives only "knowledge" of sin. In order to better grasp the position of the Law in the sin-death sequence—which is independent in itself, since it existed before the advent of the Law—we shall cite the relevant Pauline assertions below:

—Only through the Law comes *knowledge* of sin (3:20).

—"If it had not been for the law, I should not have *known* sin" (7:7).

—Law came in, *to increase* the trespass (5:20).

—It is the occasion for sin to *dominate* human beings (6:14).

—When the law came, sin *revived* (7:9).

—Law is the *occasion* for sin's seduction (7:11).

—It gives rise to covetousness (*epithumia*), which in turn brings about sin (7:7-8).

—It is weakened by the flesh (8:3).

The importance of the Law to justify is indicated in the first and last of the passages cited; this will set in bold relief the strength of the grace that comes to us from faith in Christ.

Paul makes two essential assertions:

a. From the time of Adam, sin (situational, non-imputable) exists in all people; this sin involves death. Thus death is not punishment for a personal sin, but is a "condemnation" in a much broader sense.

b. From the time of the Law, sin is revived, abounds, controls, seduces, or simply is "known" in all its seductive strength. Since then, the sin-death relationship which existed before the Law has undergone a modification. Now sin is culpable, and death is punishment.

The Law is the axis that determines and sustains the experience of sin and of its consequence, death. The theme of *death* is essential for Paul, because it will be his starting point for his counter-analysis of the salvific work of Christ.

What in Romans appears as an ontological status of humankind under the Law is rounded out in the Letter to the Galatians with a mention of what we might call the "hell of culpability" under the rule of the Law.

"For all who rely on works of the law—he asserts in Gal. 3:10—are *under a curse*; for it is written 'Cursed be every one who does not abide by all things written in the book of the law." Paul exploits an argument drawn from the Law, the only norm of the Jew. Human beings, then, are cursed (and deserve death) if they do not fulfill the Law *in its entirety.* But people cannot satisfy the total and unlimited requirements of the Law, above all because in the course of time it has been enlarged and extended with an infinitude of precepts and traditions. It is an inhuman task. The Law itself transforms our approximation to righteousness into distance. "The intention to reduce sin through observance becomes sin."[2]

Whence the "hell of culpability": we can be just only through the Law, but precisely through it we show ourselves to be sinners. Paul spotlights this circularity between the Law and sin: the failure of the Law's original intention (in itself it is good and holy, Rom. 7:12-16, and spiritual, 7:14); human frustration in longing for righteousness. Paul sharpens even further the crisis of the Pharisees under the Law: their *sin* does not consist only in transgressing the commandment and thus being cursed (without being able to avoid it, in fact). In addition, because of their will to save themselves by satisfying the requirements of the Law (*kaujesis,* or "ostentation"), their whole project is rendered immoral, the "work of the flesh" (Gal. 5:19; Rom. 7:5; 8:4ff.), the "desires of the flesh" (8:6ff.; Gal. 5:17ff.). The Pharisees thus condemn themselves. They try to justify themselves through the Law alone, and through it they are condemned.

These last considerations on the curse-of-Law are a profound Pauline interpretation of the human being given over to the Law as the only service of righteousness; they apply to any type of legalistic pharisaism. What we have summarized above, with respect to the "emergence" of sin since the advent of the Law, is applicable to any human situation under oppressive legal structures. The structure exhibits its inherent weakness by "giving knowledge" of sin without granting the strength to observe the law. Otherwise—and this is very common and typical—it ensures its observance through new prescriptions that depersonalize, alienate, and oppress. All of us have had the experience of this self-movement of the law in the direction of structural violence.

We must not fail to note an essential element with regard to the above. Paul testifies that the Law is the *source of sin* and that sin leads to *death*. It becomes, by the same token, a "ministry of death" (*Diakonia tou thanatou*, 2 Cor. 3:7). We must emphasize this to be able to understand the liberating action of Christ, which begins precisely at the point where this "ministry" of the Law ends. The key to everything is *death*. Sin, in itself, leads to death (for all persons, since Adam). Paul here is not making a "juridical" statement but a theological one: this is not to say that situational sin begets death as a deserved consequence; it is simply that death is implied in the *hamartia* that reigns in the world. The Law, which revives sin and makes it personal, intensifies the step toward death (now become punishment, as in Adam: Gen. 3:22ff.). The Law, which "curses" those who depend on it for support and do not observe it, destines them to death (the result of the curse). The Law, now become a "hell of culpability," again becomes a ministry of death. The Law conveys to death along any one of its channels.

But would the Law's own exhaustion, its death, be in this very "ministry"?

Before embarking on the itinerary of the New Person, beginning at this critical moment of death that separates Law and grace, let us reflect for a moment on the condition of the Person so penetratingly described by Paul.

The triple concatenation of Law-sin-death totalizes human alienation. It combines, in effect, a *present* experience (life under the Law, felt as a being-for-curse) and an anticipated frustration of being (being-for-death, lived at a new intensity). A present of anguish and an empty future, such is the living experience of the person subjected to the Law. By being delivered over to the Law, the person is also delivered to sin, in a destructive paradox.

In the Law-sin-death sequence, each element conditions the other two or is conditioned by them. This phenomenon has already been analyzed. Formulated now in other words, death is the terminus of everything, always, and a failure of the human project of justification. The Law points up the virulence of sin, which is reborn from it and changes in sign. But that which ever remains in the middle is *sin*. This is the reality that Paul continuously wishes to emphasize by demonstrating all its interlocking connections. The old person—subjected to the Law—is enslaved to *sin* (Rom. 6:6).

Thus the salvific event of Christ has its epicenter in the redemption of the *sinful* person from the greatest alienation. But because of the Law-sin-death concatenation—sin is "tied" between the other two—his grace must be a simultaneous liberation from all three. But in the work of Christ the itinerary will be reverted: *death* will be the key to all.

3. FROM DEATH TO LIFE

In Romans 5:12-21 Paul anticipated the content of Christ's paschal work by establishing an opposition between *death* (beginning with Adam but revived under the Law) and *life* (through grace and the gift of righteousness, the work of Christ, vv. 17, 18, 21). Immediately after establishing this antithetical parallel, Paul introduces the theme of resurrection, the principle of the transformation of all things, of the rise of the New Person liberated from the Law, from sin, and from death.

We believe, nevertheless, that Paul does not dwell here so much on the soteriological and liberative value of the resurrection—as he had done in Corinthians 1 (15:1ff.). Rather he elucidates why Christ emerges to life *from death*, whose fundamental impulse is not the mortal condition of the body but rather the *deadly potency of the Law*. The New Person also arises in us through a dying to sin (Rom. 6:2ff.), which, in its turn, is a radicalization of the effectiveness of the law. Through its peculiar dynamism, the Law "kills": "The very commandment which promised life proved to be death to me" (7:10). But in that process it exhausts itself, it self-destructs. And it does this in two ways. In the first place, there occurs the sequence that we have already considered: the Law "exposes" situational sin, makes us feel culpable for its transgression, and thereby makes us fall under the "curse" of the Law, which destines us for death. Christ, "born under the law" (Gal. 4:4), represents all those subject to it and takes its "curse" unto himself: "having become a curse for us" (3:13). This curse is symbolized in his crucifixion: "Cursed be every one who hangs on a tree" (3:13). The death of Christ is, therefore, the consequence of the mortal efficacy of the Law, concentrated and carried to the extreme. But after coming to death, he is raised from the dead by the Spirit and passes on to a new life (8:11). In the kingdom of the Spirit, of freedom, and of love, the Law has nothing to do. Since the action of Christ is the reverse of Adam's save that it is "much more" (cf. 5:15-17), we all pass on to the new life, and thenceforth we are beyond the reach of the Law: "For the law of the *Spirit of life* in Christ has set me *free* from the law of sin and death" (8:2). Free of the law, the kingdom of sin and death is finished. Free of the law, sin no longer finds its "occasion" to live again. At any rate, it is necessary to pass through a "death" (see below).

In the second place, Paul develops a new argument in Romans 7:1-6. The Law controls people during their lifetime; he cites the case of the marriage law that ceases to be binding on the woman upon the death of her husband. Christ also is "discharged" from the dominion of the Law at the moment of death. Paul perceives this and applies it directly to the Christian identified with Christ (7:4).

Paul intimately unites the Christ event with its mysterious extension in the Christian. The previous references already suggested this. While Christ experienced the oppression of the Law "unto death" (see Chap. V, Sec. 5), sin burdened him with us: "For our sake he made him to be sin who knew no sin, so that in him we might become the righteousness of God (2 Cor. 5:21). That is to say, this existential experience of *our* sin is assumed by Christ in his death-resurrection that liberates us.

What exactly is it that unites us to him and identifies us with his death-resurrection, *in which* we are liberated from the law and its consequences, sin and death (Rom. 8:2)? The answer is given in Rom. 6:1-11 and it is the axial presupposition of the doctrine of redemption in the other Pauline letters. Baptism is the specific issue under discussion here. It deals with nothing new, but now we understand why this passage concerning baptism appears in this precise place. First, he delineates the contrasting parallel between Adam and Christ and concludes it in 5:20-21 with a reference to grace: ". . . but where sin increased, grace abounded all the more, so that, as sin reigned in death, grace also might reign through righteousness *to eternal life* through Jesus Christ our Lord." He then immediately connects this with the rite of baptism that incorporates the Christian into the "much more" of Christ and removes him from the line of Adam.

From then on, Paul speaks *of us* but from the perspective of the salvific and liberating mystery of the death-resurrection of Christ. Thus he emphasizes the theme *of death* in his baptismal theology (6:3-4ff.). Baptism is a *homoioma*, an "assimilation" to his death, and therefore to his resurrection (6:5). All that we have noted concerning death as the liquidator of the Law, of sin, and of itself, now applies to the Christian through baptism. Although sin leads to death (8:10; 6:13), at the very moment of death one dies *to sin* (6:11) and lives for God: "But now that you have been set free from sin . . . the return you get is . . . eternal life (6:22). Therefore Paul can also point out that the Christian *dies to the Law* "through the body of Christ" (7:4), in a clear allusion to the risen body of Christ into which the Christian is "incorporated" through baptism.

What action or commitments does baptism require of us?

What are the implications of faith in Christ for "liberation"?

How must we "re-read" this liberation from the perspective of our Latin American situation?

4. OUR PASCHAL LIBERATION

a. We have just asserted that for Paul the event of the death-resurrection of Christ is a liquidation of the Law, sin, and death; death, because of the very virulence of sin—now become "sinful beyond measure" (Rom. 7:13!) through the Law—has its ultimate consequence in the body of Christ. Raised from the dead, Christ is in the realm of the Spirit, who is life and love. We, in turn, "die" to these three realities through incorporation into Christ through baptism (Rom. 6:1ff.; cf. the baptismal motifs in Gal. 2:19ff., 26ff.: "For I through the law died to the law, that I might *live* to God . . .). Some observations are in order at this point before we deal with the theology of the New Person.

The baptismal act does not magically incorporate us into the dead and risen Christ. The experience of baptism is not wholly brought to a close at that moment. Baptism bestows the "energy" of the Spirit for the day-to-day structuring of the New Person; there is a continuous growth toward the stature of the perfect Person, who is Christ (Eph. 4:13). Baptism is a "project" of the New Person, not some mystical—or even evasive—realization. It is not only a sacrament but also an act releasing and fortifying the testimonial "confession" of faith (cf. 1 John 2:27; Eph. 1:13) that is re-elaborated hermeneutically in praxis. Thus baptism must manifest itself *in life*.

The liberation that baptism makes possible is "vocational." This seems self-evident but the New Testament kerygma confirms it with its account of Jesus' baptism in the Jordan, as we have already seen (Chapter V, Sec. 1). At the time of his anointing by the Spirit, Jesus was consecrated for a prophetic mission and marked for the vocation of the "suffering Servant." And this vocation took explicit shape in his life, through his actions and his word, coming to fruition in his death-resurrection. Such must also be Christian baptism: a "vocation" to assume the authentic Christ in life to the point of maximum self-giving to one's brothers and sisters.[3]

Baptism is not an immediate liberation from sin, death, and the Law, as is also demonstrated in that dense passage of Romans (7:13–24), where Paul still *feels* the power of these three oppressive dominions. The birth of the New Person is a struggle, an effort directed against the chaotic forces that alienate the old person.

b. How does the New Person emerge? We answer forthwith: *from death.* We understand this in light of the Pauline doctrine already expounded. Christ rises up again to life from death, his extreme action. The New Person can only be one who has been "resurrected," that is, one risen from death (Rom. 6:4–8ff.). We die to sin by dying in some way or other. We die to the Law by suffering its oppression in some way or other and by "liberating" ourselves from it. We are resurrected to something new, dying to the old. In the deepest, most mysterious, and most dramatic expression, the genuine New Person is not of this life: the New Person gives up life for the love of the brothers and sisters, as so many martyrs of our present-day Latin American emancipation struggle have done, and are doing. This is a dying and a rising from the dead with Christ; this is to be truly "baptized" in Christ.

Christ, therefore, liberates us from sin, from the Law, and from death. What does each of these assertions mean? If we recall the content of these alienations (see Sec. 1 above), we will realize the incredible projection of the paschal mystery; it is an action liberating us from egoism, from oppressive structures, from despair. The New Person is capable of loving, from the love of a particular other Person (the "sacrament" of any free giving) to self-sacrifice for the cause of the oppressed. The New Person passes from the "old written code" (Rom. 7:6) of the anti-historical laws, whether ecclesiastical or social, to the freedom of the "spirit" as true children of God who can never be enslaved (Rom. 8:14ff.; Gal. 4:1-7). The free "child" possesses a critical consciousness vis-à-vis political, social, or religious realities. Free Christians have the right to criticize the Church as structure, just as they have the right to "say their word" regarding human life in all its forms. The exercise of this right is an expression of the fully assumed paschal mystery.

When we are freed from the Law, we grow in love. But we must understand, especially at this moment in history, the inverse itinerary: *because* we grow in authentic love, in commitment, we are freed from the Law. We liberate ourselves from the perspective of life, not from that of the structure itself. We know, moreover, that changes come from below, not from above; the social, political, or religious structure merely "gathers up" and moves along what is "announced" in existing situations. Again we see the circuit noted by Paul: the structure "kills" us; in our situation as oppressed people, we can be liberated by "voiding" the Law (through political or parliamentary struggle, through religious disobedience, which very often can be "critical" and salvific); and we can then collaborate in the creation of a new order. We repeat that the oppressors liberate neither themselves nor those they oppress. For Christians, this struggle and this collaboration are a consequence of their "programmatic liberation" in baptism.

It may appear strange that what has been asserted here should be deduced from paschal theology. Nevertheless, it is clear that such assertions are legitimate, if we interpret this theology from the perspective of the concrete "situations" that people live, and not from that of some unreal asceticism. "Therefore, if any one is in Christ, he is a *new creation*; the old has passed away, behold the new has come" (2 Cor. 5:17).

The New Person is free from *within* (through the love that dislodges egoism), from *without* (from the limitation and the sterility of the law), and *toward the future* (i.e., from death as ontic limit). The "liberation" expounded by Paul in Romans embraces *the whole person*—in interiority and onticity.

Here another "re-reading" of the paschal liberation is called for. This liberation is not only individual, as it is usually explained, even though there is mention of the "Mystical Body" or of the Christian community. Members of the "Mystical Body" can be perfectly individualistic. Such individualism is a defect, however, because the communitarian value of the Church-*as-people* is fundamental. We refer, in addition, to "people" in a political or ethnic sense. The peoples, the ethnic groups (Indians, blacks, social minorities that have their own communitarian expression) have the right to freedom, to "say their word," to "be more." If they are oppressed —as they are in the present-day world—they are called to liberation, to their own "Easter" that will enable them to rise up like new peoples with full recognition of their rights. Since oppressors do not liberate, Christians must side with the oppressed because it is in them that the Christ of death and resurrection is revealed. Only thus will the oppressor peoples also be liberated, by having the ground on which they move as oppressors cut from under them. This sociopolitical understanding of the New Person applies with extreme urgency to Latin America. The "baptism-vocation" of the Christian will be realized in the praxis of a liberating faith.

We speak of "vocation": the New Person is in the making. The Risen Christ *is still not* present in a world dominated by the old power structures; he is not present in the Church in complicity with the power-wielders. But he is rising up in a new Church, from the grassroots of a faith-praxis and commitment. The Risen One is appearing in struggling men and women, in *many peoples* who are dying to oppression and dependence in order to rise to their fullness of being.

5. HERMENEUTICS OF "PASCHAL" LIBERATION

How can we understand anew this triple liberation that Paul establishes as the core of the paschal mystery? If a hermeneutics geared to "unfolding" the meaning of the kerygma explores this kerygma *from* the perspective of the "situation," what are *our* paschal exigencies?

Once we have reviewed the Introduction and Chapter I above, we must see how the "core-of-meaning" of the Exodus reaches *us* by passing through the new paschal "donation-of-meaning." It does not stop on that kerygmatic *continuum*; rather it is both confirmed and reinterpreted from the perspective of the other "foci" (Genesis, prophets, Gospels) that take on a new meaning *in the perspective of* our Latin American reality.

The question that lies at the basis of these hermeneutical reflections is one that many Christians, accustomed to "one" reading of the New Testament, ask themselves: How can we understand the *spiritual* liberation that Christ made possible for us in a *political* way? In all his letters Paul simply ignores the economic and cultural orders; he dissociates the sociopolitical order from the idea of liberation when he urges slaves to remain in their condition (1 Cor. 7:20-24; 1 Tim. 6:1-2) and subjects of the Empire to obey the constituted authorities, even though they were oppressive, as we know (Rom. 13:1ff.).

We must clarify the panorama with the greatest possible clarity and simplicity.

In the first place, Paul lays the *foundation* for all liberation by emphasizing the role of the *love* of neighbor—in line with Christ's liberating actions, carried to the "limit" in his self-sacrifice unto death. Once we discover that the slave is our "brother," the relationship of domination begins to weaken, as we see in Paul's brief message to Philemon[4] and in the situation of Christian "slaves" in the Roman Empire. Paul exhorts his readers to submit to the authorities of this oppressive world, but only insofar as he considers that they exercise their power "for good." His vision is ingenuous from the sociopolitical point of view. But the fact is that the key idea of Christianity—set in boldest relief by Paul in all his letters (see especially 1 Cor. 12:3 and Eph. 4:5) namely, the confession of Christ as the only "Lord" (*Kurios*), unleashed the first "revolution" in the Empire. Christians were persecuted as "subversives" and even as "atheists" because they did not accept the cult of the emperor. These facts have a hermeneutical significance: they derive from the original meaning of the Christian kerygma, but they show, in turn, that "situations" are what liberate that meaning, previously hidden.[5]

Let us return to the question, however, because everything has not been explained.

Our first assertion is the following: when the biblical kerygma emphasizes some value, that value is never lost. Such is certainly the case as regards its deep "intentionality," though it is not necessarily so as regards its exterior or cultural contours. The Exodus has been characterized as an event of *political, social* liberation, at the *people* level, and God appeared in his act of love under the sign of the *violence-of-justice*. We have already explored the implications of that liberating moment for the people of Israel and how its deep meaning remained "recollected" in the "credos" or confessions of faith for centuries of conscientization in freedom. Among those values that of the "people" acquires a programmatic force, for human beings are liberated in communion, in dialogue with their oppressed brothers and sisters. But here something remains unrealized, as if in suspension: genuine liberation also liberates the oppressors, in a broader communion in which there are neither oppressed nor oppressors. The Exodus event did not have the historical conditions necessary to develop that "meaning"; its political urgency, moreover, delayed reflection on *other* spiritual values. But we emphasize here that in some way these other values are prefigured—if not "said" in another language—since they have their foundation in the *vocation of peoples to freedom* as a divine plan.

A second assertion: the Christ-event *subsumes and extends* the kerygma of the Exodus. How? We can see that this is so in three phenomena: the use of the lexicon of the Exodus, the marking out of new dimensions of liberation, the "exploration" meaning of the interpretation of the Exodus.

1. Paul re-reads christologically the vocabulary of the Exodus—meditated upon in turn by the "confession" of Israel in its long historical experience. Paul relates to the paschal mystery the characteristic terms of *lutroo* ("ransom/redeem"), *eleutheria* ("freedom"), *sozo* ("to save"), *hilasterion* ("propitiatory," cf. Exod. 25:17ff., in the context of the Exodus-desert), etc. Christ "redeems" us (Rom. 3:24) from sins, from slavery (cf. Exod. 20:1), from the Law (Gal. 3:13; 4:5), from death (Rom. 8). Thus the kerygma of the Exodus is incorporated into the paschal mystery, which is expressed precisely in the language of liberation, explicitly so in Romans 3-8. The "memory" of the Exodus is absorbed and integrated into the paschal "memory," as the continuity of the "paschal" language shows. Paul himself refers to Christ as "our paschal lamb" (1 Cor. 5:7). Indeed the Christian celebration is prolonging the Exodus in every eucharistic communion. What must this paschal proclamation arouse in us?

2. The actions and the word-life of Christ rediscover and liberate *human beings* oppressed by social and religious structures, giving them the possibility to "say their word." The paschal event is a "redemption" of human beings oppressed by the Law, and consequently by sin (the extreme of alienation) and the wages of sin, death (Rom. 6:23). The Old Testament is based on the rule of the Law—which is simply a "pedagogue" pointing toward Christ (Gal. 3:24). It was not able to develop this theology of liberation from structures, and had barely begun to express a faith in the resurrection. Its emphasis on forgiveness of sins (with a profound sense of "people," cf. Neh. 9, Dan.

3:24ff., etc.) would deteriorate through the "ostentation" (*kaujesis*) of pharisaic self-justification through the works of the Law. "Paschal liberation—as we have discovered in Paul—deepens that of the Exodus. The three values noted by him involve the *whole person,* in both being and vocation.

3. Thus we situate liberation in a particular cultural context (the Jewish and pharisaic world), but a context that at the same time is open (liberation from sin and death); and this liberation is guaranteed by the "memory" of the Exodus event. By so situating liberation we are able to "explore" hermeneutically its present existential and prophetic meaning.

A third assertion: today we can interpret the Exodus and the paschal mystery only *from the perspective of our situation* as dependent and oppressed peoples, or as persons dominated by the power structures. Such a context of oppression is, once again, "religious"; it is even more alienating than pharisaism because of the levers of power used. But this context is above all cultural, social, political, and economic. In Third World countries it is *politico-economic* oppression that shapes the "radical evil." This evil is the fruit of the mania to "have more" of the richer nations; it is made possible and incremented by satanic power structures. What does it mean to be a Christian in a world of dependency like this? How can Christians express—at the levels of "confession" and praxis—faith in the Risen One and in his paschal liberation? Where will the New Latin American Person come forth?

There is a dimension of *sin* that we know in the experience of our reality; *there*, in that dimension, liberation from sin, which Christ makes possible, takes place. There is a political dimension of love for our brothers and sisters oppressed by the powers of *this* world; it is *there* that *loving* Christians situate themselves. There is a political and economic death of many peoples who cannot "be more" or freely assume their historical vocation; it is *there* that the commitment of faith must be measured. There are spurious forms of expressing love (developmentalism, alliances for progress, birth control and family "planning," etc.): it is *there* that the prophetic denunciation and the conscientizing word of Christians must be heard. We could go on listing the situations of oppression that characterize the present-day world-of-sin; it is in these situations that faith has its great opportunity to be incarnated. To continue to insist on the "spiritual mission" of the church is to render a service to sin. But in fact is not liberating praxis demanded on every level by the "situation" tremendously *spiritual*? Is it not God's salvific plan to lead the whole person, as individual or as *people,* to self-fulfillment in freedom?

To believe in Christ means to act here and now within our reality.

Thus we see that the circuit we began with the Exodus continues, as a new forward movement, in our own history. For in our history we recognize anew the step of the liberator God and we confess him anew in a liberating faith-praxis. The salvation-event in the Exodus, the kerygma of the human vocation to freedom (Genesis), the prophetic denunciation of injustice, the judgment of Jesus of Nazareth against the oppressive structures of the Law, his most profound liberation in the paschal mystery: all these delineate the core of the kerygma that is intelligible to us, in Latin America, only from the perspective of their hermeneutical implications as a "historical project" of liberation.

6. CONCLUSION

To "re-read" the biblical message *from* our perspective is the only way to explore its reservoir-of-meaning. In so doing we find an answer to a question often posed in hermeneutical studies: which route is to be taken: from the biblical text to us—affirming the "us"—or from our situation back to the text, in order to illuminate the text and then return to the situation? We reply: when the "hermeneutical circularity" is profound, the distinction between the two approaches is blurred and they become simultaneous. What allows us to "enter" into the meaning of the text is the present event; from then on, even though we begin by approaching the biblical text, we are *already* "pre-understanding" it from the perspective of our existential situation, which for us Latin Americans is well known.

This explains why biblical scholars can be more or less sensitive to the liberation motifs of certain kerygmatic foci of Sacred Scripture. It also explains why these scholars prefer to explore particular biblical areas, as we have done in this essay. To raise up the liberating "memory" of so many central texts of the Bible is not a pastime but a necessary task at this particular moment.

Notes

PREFACE TO THE REVISED EDITION

1. In our opinion Juan Luis Segundo, in *The Liberation of Theology* (Maryknoll, N.Y.: Orbis Books, 1976), p. 112, did not perceive the methodological intention of our analysis in his reference to the theme.
2. See, for example, the predominant orientation of the review *Tierra Nueva* published in Bogotá, Colombia.
3. This concern with methodology constitutes the principal merit of the aforementioned work by Juan Luis Segundo. See also, Ignacio Ellacuría, "Tesis sobre posibilidad, necesidad y sentido de una teología latinoamericana," in *Teología y mundo contemporáneo* (Homage to Karl Rahner) (Madrid: Cristiandad, 1975), pp. 325-50; *Christus* (Mexico) 40 (1975): 12-16, 17-23; R. Vidales, "Cuestiones en torno al método de la teología de la liberación," in *Encuentro Latino Americano de Teología: Liberación y Cautiverio* (Mexico: Organizing Committee, 1976), pp. 225-60; in English see "Methodological Issues in Liberation Theology," in Rosino Gibellini, ed., *Frontiers of Theology in Latin America* (Maryknoll, N.Y.: Orbis Books, 1979), pp. 34-57.
4. For a more elaborate formulation, see Leonardo Boff, *Teología desde el cautiverio* (Bogotá: Indo-American Press Service, 1975); idem, "Que é fazer teologia partindo de uma América Latina en cautiveiro," *Revista Eclesiástica Brasileira* 35 (1975): 853-79 (= *Servir* 11 [1975]: 399-432).
5. Paul Ricoeur, "La función hermenéutica de la distanciación," in *Exégesis* (Buenos Aires: La Aurora, 1978).
6. Isa. 40:3 ff.; 41:17-20; 43:16-21; 51:9-11; 52:11-12.
7. See our article "Dios en el acontecimiento," *Revista Bíblica* 34 (1973):52-60.
8. On the prophetic formula "to seek God" compare, for example, Isa. 58:2: Jer. 21:2; Ezek. 14:7; 20:1; Hos. 10:12; Amos 5:4.
9. See a synthesis of the problematic in Jürgen Moltmann, "Carta abierta a José Míguez Bonino," *Cuadernos de Teología* 4 (1975): 188-96; published in English in *Christianity and Crisis*, March 29, 1976.

CHAPTER I

1. Hans-Georg Gadamer, *Truth and Method* (New York: Seabury, 1975), pp. 267-69. Cf. Emerich Coreth, *Cuestiones fundamentales de hermenéutica* (Barcelona: Herder, 1972), pp. 161 ff.
2. Ricoeur, "La función hermenéutica." In this study, Ricoeur extends and corrects Gadamer.
3. See P. Lapointe, *Les trois dimensions de l'hermenéutique* (Paris: Gabalda, 1968); for an evaluation, see J. I. Vicentini and A. Levoratti, *Mito y hermenéutica* (Buenos Aires: El Escudo, 1973), pp. 11-29.
4. Paul Ricoeur, *The Conflict of Interpretations: Essays in Hermeneutics* (Evanston, Ill.: Northwestern University Press, 1974), "Structure, Word, Event," pp. 79-96. Idem, "La función hermenéutica," sec. 3, "El discurso como obra"; sec. 4, "El mundo de la obra"; sec. 5, "Comprenderse delante de la obra."
5. Hugo Assmann, "Implicaciones socioanalíticas e ideológicas del lenguaje de liberación," in the anthology *Pueblo oprimido, señor de la historia* (Montevideo: Tierra Nueva, 1972), pp. 161-71; P. Negre Rigol, "Los cambios metodológicos de las ciencias sociales y la interpretación

teológica," ibid., pp. 177-96 (both articles with bibliography). The analysis by Franz J. Hinkelammert, *Las armas ideológicas de la muerte* (San José de Costa Rica: Educa, 1977), also merits consideration.

6. See Paulo Freire, *Pedagogy of the Oppressed,* trans. Myra B. Ramos (New York: Herder and Herder, 1970), chap. 1.

7. For the contribution of these three men to an exposure of the "illusion" of the subject, or self-consciousness, see Paul Ricoeur, "Psychoanalysis and the Movement of Contemporary Culture," in *The Conflict of Interpretations,* pp. 121-59.

8. For a synthetized treatment of this point, see "La lectura cristiana de los signos de los tiempos," *Teología* 5 (1967): 49-60.

9. In the area of exegesis, see Lapointe, *Trois dimensions.* In regard to the philosophy of language, see Paul Ricoeur, "Evénement et sens," *Archivio de Filosofía* (1971):5-37.

10. Among the numerous studies dealing with this reality of Brazilian Christianity, see above all the anthology *Comunidades eclesiais de base: Uma igreja que nasce do povo* (Petrópolis: Vozes, 1975); Leonardo Boff, *Eclesiogênese: as comunidades eclesiais de base reinventam a igreja* (Petrópolis: Vozes, 1977); J. Ramalho, "CEB: nova forma participatoria do povo," SEDOC 9 (1976); A. Ribeiro Guimaraes, "Comunidades eclesiasis de base: busca de equilibrio entre ministerios e comunidade cristã," *Revista Eclesiástica Brasileira* 18 (1978):80-102 (Ministries in the Church arise from the community, ecclesiology develops from ecclesiogenesis). For a more complete bibliography, consult the *Bibliografía Teológica Comentada* published yearly by the Instituto Superior Evangélico de Estudios Teológicos (ISEDET) of Buenos Aires (Camacúa 282, 1406 Buenos Aires), in section 2.2 ("Comunidades de base"). See also the reflections of theologians and pastors of the Regional Nordeste II of the CNBB, in "América Latina, Boletín" (MIEC-JECI), no. 25 (Lima, February 1978), pp. 14-22.

11. See Enrique Dussel, *Historia de la Iglesia en América Latina* (Barcelona: Nova Terra, 1972), passim.

CHAPTER II

1. See our *Historia de la salvación,* rev. ed. (Buenos Aires: Paulinas, 1980), chapters 2 and 3.

2. Gustavo Gutiérrez, *A Theology of Liberation* (Maryknoll, N.Y.: Orbis Books, 1973), pp. 155-59; all the articles in *Revista Bíblica* 32, no. 139 (1971) are on Exodus/Liberation; Julio de Santa Ana, "Notas para una ética de la liberación a partir de la Biblia," in *Pueblo oprimido, señor de la historia,* pp. 113-25, especially pp. 118 ff.

3. Eduardo Galeano, *Las venas abiertas de América Latina* (Mexico City: Siglo XXI, 1971), p. 106 n.28; Eng trans: *Open Veins of Latin America: Five Centuries of the Pillage of a Continent,* trans. Cedric Belfrage (New York: Monthly Review Press, 1973).

4. Freire, *Pedagogy of the Oppressed,* pp. 49-51; also *La educación como práctica de la libertad* (Buenos Aires: Siglo XXI, 1972), pp. 37 ff.

5. Galeano, *Venas abiertas,* pp. 76f. S. Trinidad, "Cristologia, conquista, colonización," *Cristianismo y Sociedad* 13 (1975): 12-28.

6. Recall the dramatic accusation symbolized in the film *Sangre de Condor* of the Bolivian Jorge Sanjines; see also "Esterilización en vez de reforma agraria," *Diálogo* (Guatemala), no. 22 (1975):25.

7. The myth has been newly translated: Wilfred G. Lambert and A. R. Millard, eds. *Atrahasis: The Babylonian Story of the Flood* (Oxford: Oxford University Press, 1969).

8. See the denunciation in "El grito del obispo," *Víspera,* no. 27 (1972):17-19; Galeano, *Venas abiertas,* pp. 208ff., "Ahora en Honduras," *Contacto* 12 (1975): 69-78, etc.

9. Freire, *Pedagogy of the Oppressed,* pp. 31-33.

10. See Paul Ricoeur, "El conflicto, ¿signo de contradicción y de unidad?" *Criterio,* no. 1668 (May 4, 1973): 252-58. especially p. 254 (the ideology of conciliation at any price); Juan Luis Segundo, "Conversão e reconciliação na perspectiva da moderna teología da libertação," *Perspectiva Teológica* 7 (1975): 162-78 (= *Cristianismo y Sociedad* 13 [1975]: 17-25); G. Ruiz, "Año jubilar hebreo y año santo cristiano: Cómo se puede espiritualizar una reconciliación y reforma social," *Diálogo,* no. 22 (1975): 11-22.

11. See J. Severino Croatto, "La función del poder ¿salvífica u opresora?" *Revista Bíblica* 33 (1972):99-106; J. Graciarena, *Poder y clases sociales en el desarrollo de América Latina* (Buenos Aires: Paidós, 1967).

CHAPTER III

1. A more detailed commentary can be found in our work, *El hombre en el mundo,* vol. 1, *Creación y designio* (Buenos Aires: La Aurora, 1974), chap. 9 ("El hombre-imagen").
2. For various studies on the function of the king, see the anthology *La regalità sacra* (Leiden: Brill, 1955); M. J. Seux, *Epithétes royales akkadiennes et sumériennes* (Paris: Letouzey et Ané, 1967).
3. See Croatto, "El Mesias liberador de los probres," *Revista Bíblica* 31 (1970): 233-40.
4. See T. Todorov, "L'analyse littéraire du récit," *Communications* 8 (1966); idem, "Poética," in the anthology, *¿Qué es el estructuralismo?* (Buenos Aires: Losada, 1971), pp. 101-73; C. Bremond, "Le message narratif," *Communications* 4 (1964).
5. Freire, *Pedagogy of the Oppressed,* p. 28; idem, *¿Extensión o comunicación?* (Buenos Aires: Siglo XXI, 1973), chap. 2.
6. Paul Ricoeur, *Freedom and Nature: The Voluntary and the Involuntary,* trans. E. V. Kovak (Evanston, Ill.: Northwestern University Press, 1966), pp. 448-50.
7. See "Notas sobre la economía y el desarrollo en América Latina," Boletín de la CEPAL, no. 88 (November 16, 1971) (Santiago de Chile); Gunnar Myrdal, *An Asian Drama: An Inquiry into the Poverty of Nations* (New York: Pantheon, 1968); R. Haan, "¡Aclara la ciencia económica el concepto de pobreza?" *Cuadernos de Teología* 5 (1977):24-47.

CHAPTER IV

1. Cf. R. Concatti, "Profetismo y política," *Nuevo Mundo* 2 (1972):90-108, and above all the conclusions arrived at in a seminar on "Prophesy today in Latin America," *Cristianismo y Sociedad* 15 (1977):3-25; E. García Ahumada, "Palabra ideológica y palabra profética," *Mensaje* 24 (1975):343-52.
2. See the excellent commentary by Rodolfo Obermuller, "¿Dónde estuviste?" *Revista Bíblica* 35 (1973):14-21.
3. Freire, *La educación como práctica de la libertad,* pp. 59 ff.
4. José Comblin, "El tema de la liberación en el pensamiento cristiano latinoamericano." *Pasos,* no. 7 (1972): 8 ff; Hugo Assmann, "El cristianismo, su plusvalía ideológica y el costo social de la revolución socialista," *Pasos,* no. 11 (1972): 12 ff. This theme is taken up again in *Teología desde la praxis de la liberación* (Salamanca: Sigueme), pp. 171-202; in English see Assmann's *Theology for a Nomad Church,* trans. Paul Burns (Maryknoll, N.Y.: Orbis Books, 1976).
5. We have amplified this problematic in "La religiosidad popular: un intento de problematización," *Cristianismo y sociedad* 14 (1976): 39-48, and "Cultura popular y projecto histórico," *Cuadernos Salmantinos de Filosofía* 3 (1976): 367-78.

CHAPTER V

1. See Martín Avanzo, "El compromiso con el necesitado en el judaismo y en el evangelio," *Revista Bíblica* 35 (1973):23-41.
2. See Freire, *Pedagogy of the Oppressed,* p. 183.
3. For the justification of this exegesis, see our *Historia de la salvación* (Buenos Aires: Paulinas, 1980), chap. 12, part 2.
4. See J. Dupont, *Les béatitudes,* vol. 2 (Paris: Gabalda, 1969); it is a noteworthy commentary.
5. Cf. Ignace de la Potterie, "Jesús roi et juge, d'aprés Jn. 19.13," *Bíblica* 41 (1960):217-47.
6. The essay by Oscar Cullmann, *Jesus and the Revolutionaries,* trans. Gareth Putnam (New York: Harper & Row, 1970), in which he discusses Jesus' membership in the Zealot movement, is well-known. Consult also the source study by Martín Avanzo, "El arresto, el juicio y la condena de Jesús: Historia y presente," *Revista Bíblica* 35 (1973):131-50 (it spotlights the intrigues of the *religious* groups, above all the scribes and the Sadducees). Jorge Pixley has written an excellent essay, *Reino de Dios* (Buenos Aires: La Aurora, 1977), in which he analyzes the development of the theme of "kingdom of God," its political and liberationist implications, the attitude of Jesus vis-à-vis the temple as a center of exploitation, and vis-à-vis the religious and political groups,

and the further transformation of his message into a universal, spiritual, and individualistic religion that has been handed down to us through the work of its interpreters. Jesus clearly distinguished himself from the Zealots.

7. Paul W. Walaskay, "The Trial and Death of Jesus in the Gospel of Luke," *Journal of Biblical Literature* 94 (1975):81-93. (Luke distorts the religious and Roman trial; Pilate favors Jesus and, even though he condemns him, is benign with him. In this manner Luke wishes to gain Roman favor toward Christians.)

8. Cullmann, *Jesus and the Revolutionaries*, and *Estudios de teología bíblica* (Madrid: Studium, 1973).

9. Jürgen Moltmann, *The Crucified God: The Cross of Christ as the Foundation and Criticism of Christian Theology* (New York: Harper & Row, 1974), pp. 139-42.

10. See note 10, in chap. 2 above.

11. Avanzo, "El arresto," pp. 137 ff., where he clarifies the false perspective that includes the Pharisees in the judgment of Jesus (John 18:3 would be an anachronism or, as we would say, a re-reading).

12. On the symbolical order and its ideological or political manipulation, see the analysis by Fernando Belo, *Lecture matérialiste de évangile de Marc* (Paris: Cerf, 1974); an English translation has been published by Orbis Books.

13. Hugo Assmann, "Medellín: el fracaso de una illusión," *Cristianismo y Sociedad* 12 (1974):137-43; F. Malley, "Un nueveo lenguaje en la iglesia de América Latina?" *Víspera* 8 (1975). In the face of the attempt to produce a "counter-reading" of Medellín, the preparatory document drawn up at Puebla was the subject of much criticism. To cite some examples: C. Boff, "A ilusão de una Nova Cristandade, Crítica a tese central de documento de consulta para Puebla," *Revista Eclesiástica Brasileira* 38 (1978):5-71; Theologians of CLAR, "Análise crítica da revelacão e da eclesiologia no documento de consulta," ibid., pp. 33-42; Pablo Richard, 1959-1978, "La iglesia latinoamericana entre el temor y la esperanza" in *Documentos DOCET* (Lima: CELADEC, 1978), no. 7, pp. 2-5 (and the other studies in this publication).

14. For the purpose of situating the hermeneutical method, the objective of this little book, see also "Las estructuras de poder en la Bíblia: La recontextualización hermenéutica," *Revista Bíblica* 37 (1975):115-28.

It is useful to note that liberation theology places a special emphasis on the historical Jesus as an expression of a liberative christology (without thereby denying the Paschal mystery; see our following chapter). See especially Jon Sobrino, "El Jesús historico, crisis y desafío para la fe," *Christus* 40 (1975):6-18; R. Vidales, "La práctica histórica de Jesús: Notas provisorias," ibid., pp. 43-55; "¿Quién es Jesucristo hoy en América Latina?" *Cristianismo y Sociedad* 13, nos. 43-44 and 46 (1975); Jon Sobrino, *Cristología desde América Latina* (Mexico: CRT, 1976); in English see Sobrino's *Christology at the Crossroads*, trans. John Drury (Maryknoll, N.Y.: Orbis Books, 1978); Leonardo Boff, "Jesus Cristo libertador: Uma visão cristológica a partir de periferia," *Revista Eclesiástica Brasileira* 37 (1977):501-24; in English see Boff's *Jesus Christ Liberator*, trans. Patrick Hughes (Maryknoll, N.Y.: Orbis Books, 1978).

CHAPTER VI

1. Paul Ricoeur, *The Symbolism of Evil*, trans. Emerson Buchanan, Religious Perspectives Series (Boston: Beacon, 1969), pp. 118-39.

2. Ibid., p. 143.

3. Enrique Dussel, *History and the Theology of Liberation: A Latin American Perspective* (Maryknoll, N.Y.: Orbis Books, 1976), p. 123 (love is genuine if it is efficacious).

4. See the interpretation of José I. Vicentini, "¿Pablo revolucionario? pero ¿como? La esclavitud según la carta a Filemón," *Revista Bíblica* 33 (1971): 43-54.

5. On this theme see our "Las estructuras de poder en la Bíblia."

Scriptural Index

Genesis
1:1 — *34*
1:26 — *31, 32, 33, 34*
1:26ff. — *35, 37*
1:28 — *33, 34*
2:5ff. — *35*
3:4 — *69*
3:22ff. — *74*
4:17-22 — *33*
5:1-3 — *32*
12:1ff. — *15*

Exodus
1-15 — *12, 26*
1:5 — *16*
1:7 — *18*
1:9 — *18*
1:9f. — *19*
1:11 — *16, 18*
1:12 — *16*
1:15ff. — *18*
3 — *15, 20*
3:6ff. — *17*
3:7 — *17, 18*
3:7-9 — *20*
3:8 — *20*
3:9 — *17, 18*
3:11 — *21*
3:13 — *21*
3:18 — *29*
3:19 — *29*
4:1 — *21*
4:10 — *21*
4:13 — *21*
4:31 — *21*
5:1 — *29*
5:1-5 — *21*
5:6-19 — *21*
5:20ff. — *21*
5:22ff. — *22*
6 — *15, 20*
6:1-13 — *18*
6:4-5 — *12*
6:4-8 — *20*
6:5 — *17, 18, 20*
6:6 — *29*
6:6ff. — *20*
6:7 — *20*
6:9 — *17, 27*
7-11 — *21*
7:4 — *29*
8:11 — *22*
8:27f. — *22*
9:34f. — *22*
10:11 — *22*
10:20 — *22*
12-15 — *23*
12:1ff. — *25*
12:14 — *23, 35*
12:17 — *23, 25, 35*
12:27 — *23*
12:29-33 — *23*
12:42 — *23*
12:51 — *23*
14:5 — *24*
14:9f. — *24*
14:11ff. — *24*
14:28 — *24*
14:31 — *24*
15 — *24, 25*
15:1 — *25*
15:1-4 — *25*
19:4 — *69*
20:1 — *80*
20:11 — *35*
20:12 — *35*
25ff. — *44*
25:17ff. — *80*
31:17 — *35*

Leviticus
14:19 — *50*
25:39ff. — *36*
25:44 — *36*

Numbers
21:10-35 — *14*

Deuteronomy
1-11 — *12*
5:15 — *35*
6:20ff. — *27*
15:7ff. — *51*
15:15 — *36*
15:21ff. — *36*
16 — *35*
16:12 — *35*
26:5ff. — *27*
29:1ff. — *69*
32:6 — *13*

Joshua
9:23 — *36*
9:27 — *36*
23:3 — *69*
24:2-13 — *27*

1 Kings
18:36 — *41*

2 Kings
24:14 — *51*

Nehemiah
9 — *80*

Psalms
119 — *69*
135:10-12 — *14*

Isaiah
1:11-17 — *44*
1:11ff. — *45*
1:21-23 — *42*
3:12 — *42*
3:12-26 — *42*
3:14ff. — *42*
5:1ff. — *42*
5:8 — *42*
9:5-7 — *56*
11:1-9 — *56*
11:4 — *56*
40:3f. — *83*
40:18ff. — *20*
41:17-20 — *83*
42:1 — *49*
42:1-4 — *48*
43:16-21 — *80*
44:21-24 — *13*
49:1 — *15*
49:1-13 — *48*
49:5 — *15*
50:4-9 — *49*
51:9-11 — *13, 83*

Scriptural Index

52:11-12	83	4:1-5	41	14:1-2	58
52:13-53:12	49	5:4	83	14:53ff.	58
54:5	13	5:7	41	14:61	49
58:2	83	5:10-13	41	14:61ff.	58
		5:21	52	14:62	49
Jeremiah		5:21-27	44	15:1	59
1:4f.	15	9:7ff.	7	15:3	59
1:9f.	40			15:4	59
2	42	**Micah**		22:66-71	59
2:2-3	40	6:3-5	41	22:70ff.	59
2:5ff.	41	6:6-7	44	23:1-2	59
2:6	44				
2:7	44	**Matthew**		**Luke**	
2:13	41, 44	5:1ff.	56	1:26ff.	15
3ff.	42	5:3-12	56	6:20-23	56
5:26ff.	43	5:17	65	7:47	70
7:1ff.	42	7:21	4	9:58	56
7:2ff.	43, 44	9:2	50	11:56	8
7:5ff.	43	9:13	70	13:34f.	60
18:21f.	43	11:1-6	51	16:19-31	56
21:2	83	11:5ff.	51	20:1ff.	58
22:3f.	42	12	52	20:19-26	59
22:12	42	12:1-8	52	20:20	59
22:16	42	12:7	52	22:27	56
22:16f.	42	12:9-14	53	23:3	59
23:3-8	56	12:10	53	23:4	59
23:9ff.	44	12:12	53	23:5	59
23:17	44	12:13	53	23:10	61
25:3ff.	28	12:14	53, 58	23:14	60
26:2ff.	44	12:14-27	49	23:20	60
28	44	12:22-30	53	23:22	60
28:1ff.	44	12:23	53		
28:9	44	12:24	54	**John**	
31:9	32	12:24-30	54	2:19	58
36:23	42	12:28	54	4	54
36:27	42	12:31ff.	52, 54	4:9	54
36:30	42	12:38ff.	52, 54	4:16ff.	54
		12:41	54	4:18	55
Ezekiel		15:1-20	54	4:25ff.	55
14:7	83	15:4-6	54	4:39	55
16:14ff.	41	18:1-11	51	5:14	50
20:1	83	21:23	58	5:17	49, 50
23:1ff.	41	23:3	71	5:18	50, 58
34:23-27	56	25:31-46	10	5:43ff.	28
		25:37ff.	43	7:1	58
Daniel		26:59-60	58	7:25	58
3:24ff.	80-81	26:61	58	7:44ff.	58
7:13ff.	49	26:63	58	8:32	67
		27:20	61	8:37	58
Hosea		27:40	58	8:44	68
1:2	41			8:55	68
2:1ff.	41	**Mark**		9	55
6:6	44, 52	1:22-27	60	9:2	50, 51
10:12	83	8:29	49	9:14	55
11:1	32	8:30	49	9:16	55
		8:31ff.	49	9:18	55
Amos		11:18	58	9:24	55
1:1-2:3	41	11:27ff.	58	9:28ff.	55
2:7	41	12	58	9:33	55
2:9ff.	41	12:12	58	9:34	55

9:35ff.	55	5:13	71, 72	8:10	76
9:39	55	5:14	71, 72	8:14ff.	77
9:40	55	5:14ff.	71	13:1ff.	79
9:41	55	5:15	72		
10:31	58	5:15-17	72	**1 Corinthians**	
14:21	67	5:15-19	72	5:7	80
15:1-16	49	5:16	72	7:20-24	79
16:12-15	67	5:17	72, 75	12:3	79
18:3	86	5:18	72, 75	15:1ff.	75
18:30	60	5:19	72		
18:36ff.	60	5:20	72	**2 Corinthians**	
19:7	58	5:20-21	76	3:7	74
19:11	60	5:21	71, 75	5:17	78
19:12	60	6:1ff.	76	5:21	75
19:13	60, 85	6:1-11	76	8:9	69
19:14	60	6:2ff.	75		
19:15	60	6:3-4ff.	76	**Galatians**	
19:22	60	6:4-8ff.	77	1:15	15
		6:5	76	2:19ff.	76
Acts		6:6	74	2:26ff.	76
2:1ff.	67	6:11	76	3:10	73
2:16ff.	46	6:13	76	3:13	75, 80
7:20ff.	28	6:14	72	3:24	80
7:35f.	28	6:22	76	4:1-7	77
7:51ff.	28	6:23	80	4:4	75
10:34ff.	67	7:1-6	75	4:5	80
15:7-11	67	7:4	75, 76	5:15-17	75
		7:5	73	5:17ff.	73
Romans		7:6	77	5:19	73
1-11	7	7:7	72	8:2	75
1:16-17	67	7:7-8	72	8:11	75
1:18	7	7:9	72		
1:18-3:20	68	7:10	75	**Ephesians**	
3-8	80	7:11	72	1:13	77
3:20	72	7:12-16	73	1:14	39
3:21f.	67	7:13	76	4:5	79
3:21-8:3	68	7:13-24	77	4:13	76
3:23	68	7:14	73		
3:24	80	7:20	72	**1 Timothy**	
4:12	68	8	80	6:1-2	79
5-8	72	8:2	76		
5:12	71, 72	8:3	72	**1 John**	
5:12-21	74	8:4ff.	73	2:27	77
		8:6ff.	73		

www.ingramcontent.com/pod-product-compliance
Lightning Source LLC
Chambersburg PA
CBHW070323100426
42743CB00011B/2539